Principles of Accounting.com

Financial Accounting Workbook

2020 Edition

Larry M. Walther
Utah State University

principlesofaccounting.com

Table of Contents

The Accounting Cycle

Current Assets

Long-Term Assets

Liabilities and Equities

Using Accounting Information

Chapter 1 Worksheets

Basic Worksheets

(a)

(b)

(c)

(d)

(e)

(a)   Cash

Asset

(b)   Dividend to shareholders

(c)   Land

(d)   Accounts payable

(e)   Capital stock

(f)   Notes payable

(g)   Accounts receivable

(h)   Salaries

(i)   Rent paid

(j)   Cost of utilities used

(k)   Customer order not yet filled

(l)   The value of completed services provided to customers

(m)   Obligation to pay for utilities consumed

		Assets	Liabilities	Equity
(a)	Paid the current month's rent.	Decrease	No Change	Decrease
(b)	Provided services to customers for cash.			
(c)	Provided services to customers on account.			
(d)	Recorded receipt of an electric bill to be paid next month.			
(e)	Paid an electric bill received in a prior month.			
(f)	Purchased land for cash.			
(g)	Purchased equipment in exchange for a note payable (loan).			
(h)	Collected a previously recorded account receivable.			
(i)	Purchased a building by paying 20% in cash and agreeing to pay the remainder over future years.			
(j)	Declared and paid a dividend to shareholders.			

Impact of transactions on fundamental accounting equation

B-01.03

(a)   The monthly fee paid to maintain Goudar's website.

       Expense

(b)   Needles, bags, plastic bandages, etc. that were used to collect blood.

(c)   Needles, bags, plastic bandages, etc. that will be used in the future to collect blood.

(d)   Amounts received from hospitals to pay for the blood products.

(e)   A loan that is owed to a bank.

(f)   The building and equipment that serves as the home office for Goudar.

(g)   Amounts owed to a printing company that prepared T-shirts given away at a recent blood drive campaign.

(h)   The salaries of employees of Goudar.

	Dec. 31, 20X1	Dec. 31, 20X2
Total Assets	$1,500,000	$2,300,000
Total Liabilities	700,000	1,400,000
Total Equity	$	$

Ending equity	$
Beginning equity	
Change in equity	$

(a)   Magee paid no dividends, and no additional capital was raised via share issuances.

(b)   Magee paid $100,000 in dividends, and no additional capital was raised via share issuances.

(c)   Magee paid no dividends, but raised $250,000 via issuances of additional shares of stock.

(d)   Magee paid $100,000 in dividends, and raised $250,000 via issuances of additional shares of stock.

CUE CORPORATION
Income Statement
for the Years Ending December 31, 20XX

	20X4		20X3		20X2	
Revenues						
Services to customers		$200,000		?		$100,000
Expenses						
Wages	?		$117,000		?	
Interest	3,000	?	3,000	?	5,000	?
Net income		?		$ 40,000		?

CUE CORPORATION
Statement of Retained Earnings
for the Years Ending December 31, 20XX

	20X4	20X3	20X2
Beginning retained earnings	?	?	$ 0
Plus: Net income	?	40,000	?
	?	?	$25,000
Less: Dividends	30,000	?	?
Ending retained earnings	$60,000	?	?

CUE CORPORATION
Balance Sheet
December 31, 20XX

	20X4		20X3		20X2	
Assets						
Cash		?		?		$ 50,000
Accounts receivable		65,000		50,000		?
Land		180,000		180,000		180,000
Total assets		?		$289,000		?
Liabilities						
Interest payable	?		$ 1,000		$ 2,000	
Loan payable	10,000		?		?	
Total liabilities		$ 11,000		$ 31,000		?
Stockholders' equity						
Capital stock	?		?		$228,000	
Retained earnings	?		30,000		?	
Total stockholders' equity		?		?		238,000
Total liabilities and equity		$299,000		?		$300,000

(a)

(b)

(c)

(a)   The fundamental accounting equation precludes a situation where liabilities exceed assets.

          Disagree

(b)   A complete set of financial statements would include a cash flow statement.

(c)   The balance sheet can be prepared in a vertical or horizontal format.

(d)   The period of time covered by each financial statement is identical.

(e)   Many assets are reported at their historical cost.

(f)   Revenue should not be recognized before it is collected.

(g)   The term income is synonymous with the term revenue.

(h)   Dividends are reported as an expense on the income statement.

(i)   Retained earnings will equal cash on hand.

(j)   Issuing stock does not increase a company's revenue or income.

COMPANY A

COMPANY B

COMPANY C

COMPANY D

Involved Worksheets

(a)

(b)

(c)

(a)

(b)

(c)

BISCEGLIA COMPANY
Income Statement

Revenues

    Services to customers

Expenses

    _____ -   _____ -

    $ _____ -

BISCEGLIA COMPANY

    _____ -

    _____ -

Ending retained earnings $ _____ -

Assets

    _____ -

Total assets $ _____ -

Liabilities

    _____ -

Total liabilities

Stockholders' equity

    _____ -

Total stockholders' equity   _____ -

Total liabilities and equity $ _____ -

Moderately complex assessment to determine income for four years | *I-01.04*

20X1

20X2

20X3

20X4

Analysis of impact of transactions on complete financial statements

BINGO CORPORATION
Income Statement
For the Month (through transaction #1)

Revenues

   Services to customers $ -

Expenses

   Wages $ -

   Utilities   -   -

Net income $ -

BINGO CORPORATION
Statement of Retained Earnings
For the Month (through transaction #1)

Beginning retained earnings $ -

Plus: Net income   -

    $ -

Less: Dividends   -

Ending retained earnings $ -

BINGO CORPORATION
Balance Sheet
As of Completion of Transaction #1

Assets

   Cash $ -

   Accounts receivable   -

   Building   -

Total assets $ -

Liabilities

   Wages payable $ -

   Notes payable   -

Total liabilities $ -

Stockholders' equity

   Capital stock $ -

   Retained earnings   -

Total stockholders' equity   -

Total liabilities and equity $ -

BINGO CORPORATION
Income Statement
For the Month (through transaction #2)

Revenues

    Services to customers $ -

Expenses

    Wages $ -

    Utilities   -   -

Net income $ -

BINGO CORPORATION
Statement of Retained Earnings
For the Month (through transaction #2)

Beginning retained earnings $ -

Plus: Net income   -

     $ -

Less: Dividends   -

Ending retained earnings $ -

BINGO CORPORATION
Balance Sheet
As of Completion of Transaction #2

Assets

    Cash $ -

    Accounts receivable   -

    Building   -

Total assets $ -

Liabilities

    Wages payable $ -

    Notes payable   -

Total liabilities $ -

Stockholders' equity

    Capital stock $ -

    Retained earnings   -

Total stockholders' equity   -

Total liabilities and equity $ -

BINGO CORPORATION
Income Statement
For the Month (through transaction #3)

Revenues

    Services to customers $ -

Expenses

    Wages $ -

    Utilities   -   -

Net income $ -

BINGO CORPORATION
Statement of Retained Earnings
For the Month (through transaction #3)

Beginning retained earnings $ -

Plus: Net income   -

                                            $ -

Less: Dividends   -

Ending retained earnings $ -

BINGO CORPORATION
Balance Sheet
As of Completion of Transaction #3

Assets

    Cash $ -

    Accounts receivable   -

    Building   -

Total assets $ -

Liabilities

    Wages payable $ -

    Notes payable   -

Total liabilities $ -

Stockholders' equity

    Capital stock $ -

    Retained earnings   -

Total stockholders' equity   -

Total liabilities and equity $ -

BINGO CORPORATION
Income Statement
For the Month (through transaction #4)

Revenues

Services to customers $ -

Expenses

Wages $ -

Utilities - -

Net income $ -

BINGO CORPORATION
Statement of Retained Earnings
For the Month (through transaction #4)

Beginning retained earnings $ -

Plus: Net income -

$ -

Less: Dividends -

Ending retained earnings $ -

BINGO CORPORATION
Balance Sheet
As of Completion of Transaction #4

Assets

Cash $ -

Accounts receivable -

Building -

Total assets $ -

Liabilities

Wages payable $ -

Notes payable -

Total liabilities $ -

Stockholders' equity

Capital stock $ -

Retained earnings -

Total stockholders' equity -

Total liabilities and equity $ -

BINGO CORPORATION
Income Statement
For the Month (through transaction #5)

Revenues

   Services to customers $ -

Expenses

   Wages $ -

   Utilities   -   -

Net income $ -

BINGO CORPORATION
Statement of Retained Earnings
For the Month (through transaction #5)

Beginning retained earnings $ -

Plus: Net income   -

                                      $ -

Less: Dividends   -

Ending retained earnings $ -

BINGO CORPORATION
Balance Sheet
As of Completion of Transaction #5

Assets

   Cash $ -

   Accounts receivable   -

   Building   -

Total assets $ -

Liabilities

   Wages payable $ -

   Notes payable   -

Total liabilities $ -

Stockholders' equity

   Capital stock $ -

   Retained earnings   -

Total stockholders' equity   -

Total liabilities and equity $ -

BINGO CORPORATION
Income Statement
For the Month (through transaction #6)

Revenues

Services to customers		$	-

Expenses

Wages	$	-	
Utilities		-	-
Net income		$	-

BINGO CORPORATION
Statement of Retained Earnings
For the Month (through transaction #6)

Beginning retained earnings	$	-
Plus: Net income		-
	$	-
Less: Dividends		-
Ending retained earnings	$	-

BINGO CORPORATION
Balance Sheet
As of Completion of Transaction #6

Assets

Cash	$	-
Accounts receivable		-
Building		-
Total assets	$	-

Liabilities

Wages payable	$	-	
Notes payable		-	
Total liabilities		$	-

Stockholders' equity

Capital stock	$	-	
Retained earnings		-	
Total stockholders' equity			-
Total liabilities and equity		$	-

BINGO CORPORATION
Income Statement
For the Month (through transaction #7)

Revenues

Services to customers $ -

Expenses

Wages $ -

Utilities   -   -

Net income $ -

BINGO CORPORATION
Statement of Retained Earnings
For the Month (through transaction #7)

Beginning retained earnings $ -

Plus: Net income   -

                                                   $ -

Less: Dividends   -

Ending retained earnings $ -

BINGO CORPORATION
Balance Sheet
As of Completion of Transaction #7

Assets

Cash $ -

Accounts receivable   -

Building   -

Total assets $ -

Liabilities

Wages payable $ -

Notes payable   -

Total liabilities $ -

Stockholders' equity

Capital stock $ -

Retained earnings   -

Total stockholders' equity   -

Total liabilities and equity $ -

BINGO CORPORATION		
Income Statement		
For the Month (through transaction #8)		
Revenues		
Services to customers		$ -
Expenses		
Wages	$ -	
Utilities	-	-
Net income		$ -

BINGO CORPORATION	
Statement of Retained Earnings	
For the Month (through transaction #8)	
Beginning retained earnings	$ -
Plus: Net income	-
	$ -
Less: Dividends	-
Ending retained earnings	$ -

BINGO CORPORATION		
Balance Sheet		
As of Completion of Transaction #8		
Assets		
Cash		$ -
Accounts receivable		-
Building		-
Total assets		$ -
Liabilities		
Wages payable	$ -	
Notes payable	-	
Total liabilities		$ -
Stockholders' equity		
Capital stock	$ -	
Retained earnings	-	
Total stockholders' equity		-
Total liabilities and equity		$ -

BINGO CORPORATION
Income Statement
For the Month (through transaction #9)

Revenues

    Services to customers $ -

Expenses

    Wages $ -

    Utilities   -   -

Net income $ -

BINGO CORPORATION
Statement of Retained Earnings
For the Month (through transaction #9)

Beginning retained earnings $ -

Plus: Net income   -

                                    $ -

Less: Dividends   -

Ending retained earnings $ -

BINGO CORPORATION
Balance Sheet
As of Completion of Transaction #9

Assets

    Cash $ -

    Accounts receivable   -

    Building   -

    Total assets $ -

Liabilities

    Wages payable $ -

    Notes payable   -

    Total liabilities $ -

Stockholders' equity

    Capital stock $ -

    Retained earnings   -

    Total stockholders' equity   -

    Total liabilities and equity $ -

BINGO CORPORATION
Income Statement
For the Month (through transaction #10)

Revenues

   Services to customers $ -

Expenses

   Wages $ -

   Utilities   -   -

Net income $ -

BINGO CORPORATION
Statement of Retained Earnings
For the Month (through transaction #10)

Beginning retained earnings $ -

Plus: Net income   -

    $ -

Less: Dividends   -

Ending retained earnings $ -

BINGO CORPORATION
Balance Sheet
As of Completion of Transaction #10

Assets

   Cash $ -

   Accounts receivable   -

   Building   -

Total assets $ -

Liabilities

   Wages payable $ -

   Notes payable   -

Total liabilities $ -

Stockholders' equity

   Capital stock $ -

   Retained earnings   -

Total stockholders' equity   -

Total liabilities and equity $ -

I-01.06   *Computing income and extended analysis based on partial data*

    (a)   Revenue $80,000

    (b)

    (c)

Team-based identification of errors and corrections | I-01.07

(a) & (b)

Income Statement

Statement of Retained Earnings
For the Year Ending December 31, 20X5

Beginning retained earnings	$45,000

December 31, 20X5

Assets

Cash	$	92,700
Accounts receivable		37,400
Equipment		239,000
Total assets	$	369,100

Liabilities

Total liabilities	$	-

Stockholders' equity

Retained earnings		
Total stockholders' equity		-
Total liabilities and equity	$	-

(a) - (b)

SKOUSEN EXPLORATION CORPORATION
Income Statement
For the Year Ending December 31, 20X3

Revenues				
Services to customers			$	-
Expenses				
Rent	$	-		
Wages		-		
Interest		-		
Taxes		-		-
Net income			$	-

SKOUSEN EXPLORATION CORPORATION
Statement of Retained Earnings
For the Year Ending December 31, 20X3

Beginning retained earnings	$	-
Plus: Net income		-
	$	-
Less: Dividends		-
Ending retained earnings	$	-

(c) Cash received:

From customers ($1,600,000 - $125,000)	$	-		
From stockholders		-		
From lenders		-	$	-
Cash payments:				
For rent	$	-		
For wages		-		
For interest		-		
For taxes		-		
For dividends		-		
For land, building, equipment		-		
For repayment of loans		-		-
Ending cash			$	-

(d)

SKOUSEN EXPLORATION CORPORATION
Balance Sheet
December 31, 20X3

Assets

Cash	$	-
Accounts receivable		-
Land		-
Building		-
Equipment		-
Total assets	$	-

Liabilities

Rent payable	$	-
Wages payable		-
Interest payable		-
Loan payable		-
Total liabilities	$	-

Stockholders' equity

Capital stock	$	-
Retained earnings		-
Total stockholders' equity		-
Total Liabilities and equity	$	-

(a)

(b)

(c)

(d) At this point in your study, you will be challenged to prepare the following statement of cash flows! If you avoid changing the formulas in column "F" of the electronic spreadsheet, you should simplify your search for the correct answer.

HARISH COMPANY Statement of Cash Flows For the Year Ending December 31, 20X1		
Operating activities		
Cash received from customers	$ -	
Cash paid for wages	-	
Cash paid for rent	-	
Cash provided by operations		$ -
Investing activities		
Purchase of equipment	-	
Financing activities		
Issue stock	$ -	
Proceeds of loan	-	-
Increase in cash		$ -
Cash, January 1		-
Cash, December 31		$ -

(c)   Company Name:

      Revenues

      Income

      Assets

      Liabilities

Basic Worksheets

Understanding the basic "tools" of accounting B-02.01

(a)

(b)

(c)

(d)

(e)

(f)

		Increased with a:	Decreased with a:	Normal Balance:
(a)	Cash	Debit	Credit	Debit
(b)	Capital Stock			
(c)	Accounts Payable			
(d)	Revenues			
(e)	Rent Expense			
(f)	Equipment			
(g)	Dividends			
(h)	Utilities Expense			
(i)	Accounts Receivable			
(j)	Loan Payable			

GENERAL JOURNAL				Page 1
Date	Accounts		Debit	Credit
1-2-X5				
1-4-X5				
1-12-X5				
1-15-X5				
1-18-X5				
1-20-X5				
1-22-X5				

GENERAL JOURNAL				Page 2
Date	Accounts		Debit	Credit
1-23-X5				
1-25-X5				
1-31-X5				

January 2, 1961

January 3, 1961

January 5, 1961

January 7, 1961

January 8, 1961

January 9, 1961

January 11, 1961

Cash

Date	Description	Debit	Credit	Balance
01-Jan-X5	Balance forward	-	-	-
02-Jan-X5	Journal Page 1	1,000,000	-	1,000,000

Accounts Receivable

Date	Description	Debit	Credit	Balance
01-Jan-X5	Balance forward	-	-	-

Equipment

Date	Description	Debit	Credit	Balance
01-Jan-X5	Balance forward	-	-	-

Accounts Payable

Date	Description	Debit	Credit	Balance
01-Jan-X5	Balance forward	-	-	-

Loan Payable

Date	Description	Debit	Credit	Balance
01-Jan-X5	Balance forward	-	-	-

Capital Stock

Date	Description	Debit	Credit	Balance
01-Jan-X5	Balance forward	-	-	-

Revenues

Date	Description	Debit	Credit	Balance
01-Jan-X5		-	-	-

Supplies Expense

Date	Description	Debit	Credit	Balance
01-Jan-X5		-	-	-

Wage Expense

Date	Description	Debit	Credit	Balance
01-Jan-X5		-	-	-

Interest Expense

Date	Description	Debit	Credit	Balance
01-Jan-X5		-	-	-

	Debits	Credits
Cash	$ 219,000	
Accounts receivable		
Land		
Salaries payable		
Capital stock		
Revenues		
Supplies expense		
Utilities expense		
Salaries expense		
	$ -	$ -

	CASH			REVENUES	
1/1/X1	85,000			15,230	#1
#1	15,230				

	ACCOUNTS RECEIVABLE			SUPPLIES EXPENSE	
1/1/X1	54,300				

	ACCOUNTS PAYABLE			UTILITIES EXPENSE	
	31,275	1/1/X1			

The T-accounts reveal that ending Accounts Receivable amount to $, and ending Accounts

Payable amount to $.

(a) Below are the subsidiary ledgers for each customer (some data are provided):

Accounts Receivable			CUSTOMER # 1	
Date	**Description**	**Debit**	**Credit**	**Balance**
May 1	Balance forward	1,403	-	1,403
May 5	Purchase -- Journal page X	7,237	-	8,640
May 17	Payment -- Journal page X	-	1,403	7,237

Accounts Receivable			CUSTOMER # 2	
Date	**Description**	**Debit**	**Credit**	**Balance**
May 1	Balance forward	5,275	-	5,275
May 15				
May 26				

Accounts Receivable			CUSTOMER # 3	
Date	**Description**	**Debit**	**Credit**	**Balance**

Accounts Receivable			CUSTOMER # 4	
Date	**Description**	**Debit**	**Credit**	**Balance**

Accounts Receivable			CUSTOMER # 5	
Date	**Description**	**Debit**	**Credit**	**Balance**

(b) Below is the general ledger account:

Accounts Receivable				
Date	**Description**	**Debit**	**Credit**	**Balance**
01-Jan-05	Balance forward	-	-	17,225
May 5	Purchase -- Journal page X	7,237	-	24,462
May 7				

The Accounts Receivable general ledger account balance of $_____ is in agreement with the sum

of the individual subsidiary accounts ($7,237 + $_____ + $_____ + $_____ = $_____).

(c)

(d)

Customer #_____ is delinquent.

Customer #_____ 's balance exceeds the $10,000 credit limit.

Involved Worksheets

(a)

GENERAL JOURNAL				Page 1
Date	Accounts		Debit	Credit
June 2	Cash			
	Capital Stock			
	Tom Pryor invested $25,000 cash in the capital stock of the newly formed corporation.			
	Purchased (and immediately used) office supplies on account for $750.			
	Received $2,500 from Pomero for work performed to date.			
	Paid $1,200 for travel costs associated with consultation work.			
	Provided services on account to Arpy for $3,000.			
	Paid $1,500 to administrative assistant for salary.			

GENERAL JOURNAL				Page 2
Date	**Accounts**		**Debit**	**Credit**
	Billed Farris for $4,000 consulting engagement performed.			
	The company paid Tom Pryor a $1,000 dividend.			
	Collected 50% of the amount due for the billing on June 23.			
	Purchased computer furniture for $4,000, paying $1,000 down.			
	Paid $750 on the open account relating to the June 8 purchase.			
	Completed the Pomero job and billed the remaining amount.			

GENERAL JOURNAL				Page 3
Date	**Accounts**		**Debit**	**Credit**
	Paid $1,500 to administrative assistant for salary.			
	Paid rent for June, $1,000.			

(b)

Cash

Date	Description	Debit	Credit	Balance
June 1	Balance forward	-	-	-
	Journal Page 1	25,000	-	25,000

Accounts Receivable

Date	Description	Debit	Credit	Balance
June 1	Balance forward	-	-	-

Equipment

Date	Description	Debit	Credit	Balance
June 1	Balance forward	-	-	-

Accounts Payable

Date	Description	Debit	Credit	Balance
June 1	Balance forward	-	-	-

Capital Stock

Date	Description	Debit	Credit	Balance
June 1	Balance forward	-	-	-
	Journal Page 1	-	25,000	25,000

Dividends

Date	Description	Debit	Credit	Balance
June 1		-	-	-

Revenues

Date	Description	Debit	Credit	Balance
June 1		-	-	-

Salary Expense

Date	Description	Debit	Credit	Balance
June 1		-	-	-

Rent Expense

Date	Description	Debit	Credit	Balance
June 1		-	-	-

Travel Expense

Date	Description	Debit	Credit	Balance
June 1		-	-	-

Supplies Expense

Date	Description	Debit	Credit	Balance
June 1		-	-	-

(c)

TOM PRYOR CONSULTING
Trial Balance
June 30, 20XX

| | Debits | Credits |

(a)

GENERAL JOURNAL			Page	
Date	Accounts		Debit	Credit
March	Cash		30,000	
	Capital Stock			30,000
	Issue capital stock for cash			

(b)

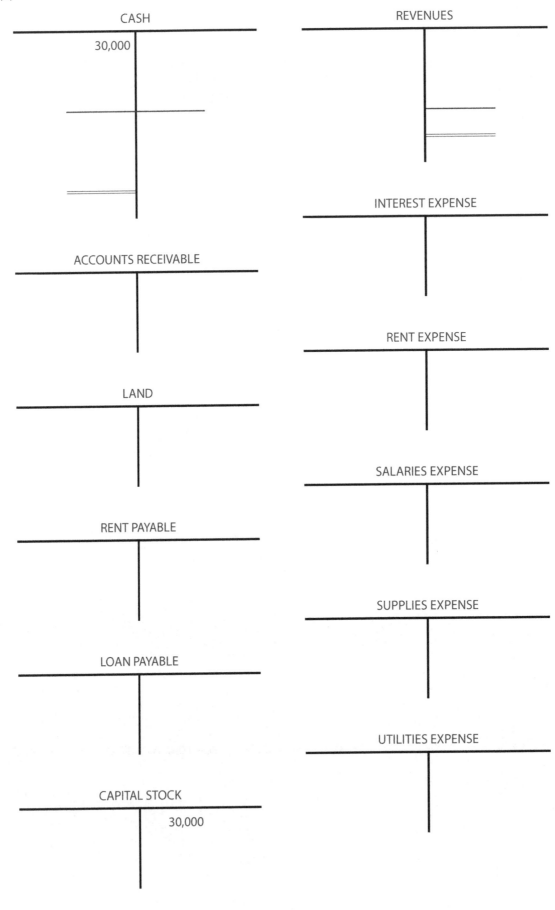

(c)

PAUL MORRIS VETERINARY Trial Balance As of March 31, 20XX		
	Debits	**Credits**
Cash	$ -	$ -
Accounts receivable	-	-
Land	-	-
Rent payable	-	-
Loan payable	-	-
Capital stock	-	-
Revenues	-	-
Interest expense	-	-
Rent expense	-	-
Salaries expense	-	-
Supplies expense	-	-
Utilities expense	-	-
	$ -	$ -

(d)

PAUL MORRIS CORPORATION
Income Statement
For the Month Ending March 31, 20XX

Revenues			
Services to customers		$	-
Expenses			
Interest	$	-	
Rent		-	
Salaries		-	
Supplies		-	
Utilities		-	-
Net income		$	-

PAUL MORRIS CORPORATION
Statement of Retained Earnings
For the Month Ending March 31, 20XX

Beginning retained earnings	$	-
Plus: Net income		-
	$	-
Less: Dividends		-
Ending retained earnings	$	-

PAUL MORRIS CORPORATION
Balance Sheet
March 31, 20XX

Assets			
Cash		$	-
Accounts receivable			-
Land			-
Total assets		$	-
Liabilities			
Rent payable	$	-	
Loan payable		-	
Total liabilities		$	-
Stockholders' equity			
Capital stock	$	-	
Retained earnings		-	
Total stockholders' equity			-
Total liabilities and equity		$	-

This problem will have many different solutions and approaches. No worksheet is provided.

(a), (c)

Cash

Date	Description	Debit	Credit	Balance
Jan. 1	Balance forward	-	-	25,000

Accounts Receivable

Date	Description	Debit	Credit	Balance
Jan. 1	Balance forward	-	-	75,000

Land

Date	Description	Debit	Credit	Balance
Jan. 1	Balance forward	-	-	150,000

Accounts Payable

Date	Description	Debit	Credit	Balance
Jan. 1	Balance forward	-	-	60,000

Loan Payable

Date	Description	Debit	Credit	Balance
Jan. 1	Balance forward	-	-	30,000

Capital Stock

Date	Description	Debit	Credit	Balance
Jan. 1	Balance forward	-	-	50,000

Retained Earnings

Date	Description	Debit	Credit	Balance
Jan. 1	Balance forward	-	-	110,000

Dividends

Date	Description	Debit	Credit	Balance
Jan. 1		-	-	-

Revenues

Date	Description	Debit	Credit	Balance
Jan. 1		-	-	-

Salaries Expense

Date	Description	Debit	Credit	Balance
Jan. 1		-	-	-

Supplies Expense

Date	Description	Debit	Credit	Balance
Jan. 1		-	-	-

Rent Expense				
Date	Description	Debit	Credit	Balance
Jan. 1		-	-	-

Interest Expense				
Date	Description	Debit	Credit	Balance
Jan. 1		-	-	-

(b)

GENERAL JOURNAL			Page 1	
Date	Accounts		Debit	Credit
Jan. 2				
Jan. 3				
Jan. 5				
Jan. 7				
Jan. 11				
Jan. 12				

GENERAL JOURNAL			Debit	Page 2 Credit
Date	Accounts		Debit	Credit
Jan. 15				
Jan. 17				
Jan. 20				
Jan. 23				
Jan. 24				
Jan. 29				

GENERAL JOURNAL				Page 3
Date	Accounts		Debit	Credit
Jan. 31				
Jan. 31				

(d)

MORGAN CORPORATION Trial Balance January 31, 20X6		
	Debits	**Credits**
Cash	$ -	$ -
Accounts receivable	-	-
Land	-	-
Accounts payable		-
Loan payable		-
Capital stock		-
Retained earnings		-
Revenues		-
Salaries expense	-	-
Supplies expense	-	-
Rent expense	-	-
Interest expense	-	-
Dividends	-	-
	$ -	$ -

(e)

MORGAN CORPORATION
Income Statement
For the Month Ending January 31, 20X6

Revenues

Services to customers		$ -

Expenses

Salaries	$ -	
Supplies	-	
Rent	-	
Interest	-	-
Net income		$ -

MORGAN CORPORATION
Statement of Retained Earnings
For the Month Ending January 31, 20X6

Beginning retained earnings	$ -
Plus: Net income	-
	$ -
Less: Dividends	-
Ending retained earnings	$ -

MORGAN CORPORATION
Balance Sheet
January 31, 20X6

Assets

Cash		$ -
Accounts receivable		-
Land		-
Total assets		$ -

Liabilities

Accounts payable	$ -	
Loan payable	-	
Total liabilities		$ -

Stockholders' equity

Capital stock	$ -	
Retained earnings	-	
Total stockholders' equity		-
Total liabilities and equity		$ -

(a)

Gross receipts as reported	$1,240,000
Fact 1: Remove stockholder investments	(150,000)
Fact 2:	
Fact 3:	
Fact 4:	
Fact 5:	
Fact 6:	
Fact 7:	
Fact 8:	
Fact 8:	
Corrected gross receipts	

(b)

GENERAL JOURNAL				Page	
Date	**Accounts**			**Debit**	**Credit**
Fact 1	Cash			150,000	
	Capital Stock				150,000
	Record stockholder investment				

GENERAL JOURNAL				Page	
Date	**Accounts**			**Debit**	**Credit**

(c)

Revenues				
Date	Description	Debit	Credit	Balance
	Balance forward	-	-	-
		-	-	-
		-	-	-
		-	-	-

WILLIAMS CORPORATION
Trial Balance
December 31, 20X1

	Debits	Credits
Cash	$ -	$ -
Accounts receivable	-	-
Land	688,004	-
Accounts payable	-	-
Loan payable		-
Capital stock	-	-
Retained earnings		-
Revenues	-	-
Wages expense	575,988	-
Supplies expense	-	-
Rent expense	-	-
Interest expense	-	-
Dividends	-	-
	$ -	$ -

Error # 1 All accounts have normal balances, but two amounts are in wrong columns!

Land and Wages Expense have both moved to the correct debit column.

Error # 2 Services provided on account for $1,500 was debited to Accounts Payable and credited to Revenues.

Error # 3 Supplies Expense of $104,300 was completely omitted from the trial balance.

Error # 4 The amount recorded for Revenues was transposed. It should have been $789,998.

Error # 5 A $5,000 shareholder investment was debited to Cash and credited to Dividends.

Error # 6 An interest payment of $1,000 was debited to Loan Payable for $100 and credited to Cash for $1,000.

THIS IS AN ELECTRONIC PROBLEM ONLY. NO BLANK WORKPAPERS ARE NECESSARY.

THE WORKSHEET IS NOT PROTECTED. IF YOU CORRUPT THE FORMULAS, JUST DOWNLOAD AGAIN AND START OVER.

(a)

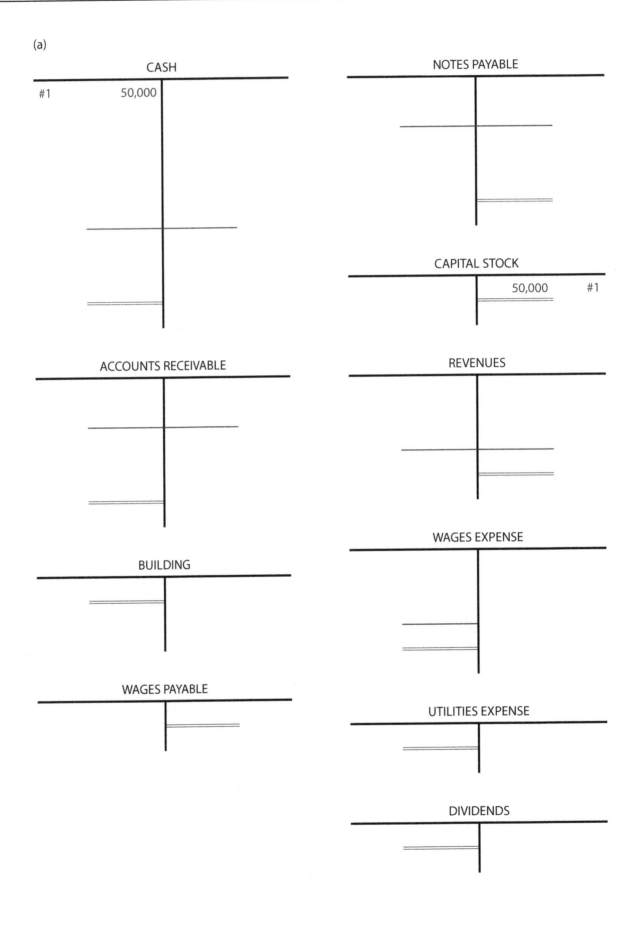

(b)

BINGO CORPORATION
Trial Balance
Month XX, 20XX

	Debits	Credits
Cash		
Accounts receivable		
Building		
Wages payable		
Note payable		
Capital stock		
Revenues		
Wages expense		
Utilities expense		
Dividends		

(c)

BINGO CORPORATION Income Statement For the Month Ending Month XX, 20XX		
Revenues		
Services to customers		$ -
Expenses		
Wages	$ -	
Utilities	-	-
Net income		$ -

BINGO CORPORATION Statement of Retained Earnings For the Month Ending Month XX, 20XX	
Beginning retained earnings	$ -
Plus: Net income	-
	$ -
Less: Dividends	-
Ending retained earnings	$ -

BINGO CORPORATION Balance Sheet Month XX, 20XX		
Assets		
Cash		$ -
Accounts receivable		-
Building		-
Total assets		$ -
Liabilities		
Wages payable	$ -	
Note payable	-	
Total liabilities		$ -
Stockholders' equity		
Capital stock	$ -	
Retained earnings	-	
Total stockholders' equity		-
Total liabilities and equity		$ -

(d)

Basic Worksheets

(1)   Depreciation

(h)   A systematic and rational allocation scheme to spread a portion of the total cost of a productive asset to each period of use.

(2)   Calendar Year

(3)   Revenue Recognition

(4)   Cash Basis

(5)   Prepaids

(6)   Unearned Revenue

(7)   Balance Sheet Approach

(8)   Adjusting Entry

(9)   Accruals

(10)   Periodicity Assumption

"NOT OK"
Revenue should not be recorded during 20X5 for the following three items:

"OK"
Revenue should be recorded during 20X5 for the following three items:

Associating cause and effect

(2)   The cost of merchandise sold to customers.

Systematic and rational allocation

Immediate recognition

GENERAL JOURNAL				
Date	**Accounts**		**Debit**	**Credit**
1-Jun				
31-Dec				

GENERAL JOURNAL				
Date	**Accounts**		**Debit**	**Credit**
various				
31-Dec				

GENERAL JOURNAL				
Date	**Accounts**		**Debit**	**Credit**
16-Dec				
31-Dec				

(a)

GENERAL JOURNAL				
Date	**Accounts**		**Debit**	**Credit**
20X1				
20X2				
20X3				
20X4				

(b), (c)

ALIDINI CORPORATION
Income Statement
For the Year Ending December 31, 20X1

...

Expenses

...

Depreciation

...

ALIDINI CORPORATION
Balance Sheet
December 31, 20X1

Assets

...

Cooling chamber

Less: Accumulated depreciation

...

ALIDINI CORPORATION
Income Statement
For the Year Ending December 31, 20X2

...

Expenses

...

Depreciation

...

ALIDINI CORPORATION
Balance Sheet
December 31, 20X2

Assets

...

Cooling chamber

Less: Accumulated depreciation

...

ALIDINI CORPORATION
Income Statement
For the Year Ending December 31, 20X3

. . .

Expenses

. . .

Depreciation

. . .

ALIDINI CORPORATION
Balance Sheet
December 31, 20X3

Assets

. . .

Cooling chamber

Less: Accumulated depreciation

. . .

ALIDINI CORPORATION
Income Statement
For the Year Ending December 31, 20X4

. . .

Expenses

. . .

Depreciation

. . .

ALIDINI CORPORATION
Balance Sheet
December 31, 20X4

Assets

. . .

Cooling chamber

Less: Accumulated depreciation   -

. . .

GENERAL JOURNAL				
Date	**Accounts**		**Debit**	**Credit**
1-Sep				
31-Dec				

GENERAL JOURNAL				
Date	**Accounts**		**Debit**	**Credit**
various				
31-Dec				

GENERAL JOURNAL				
Date	**Accounts**		**Debit**	**Credit**
16-Dec				
31-Dec				

GENERAL JOURNAL				
Date	**Accounts**		**Debit**	**Credit**
31-Dec				
31-Dec				
31-Dec				
31-Dec				

GENERAL JOURNAL				
Date	Accounts		Debit	Credit
31-Jan				
31-Jan				
31-Jan				
31-Jan				
31-Jan				
31-Jan				
31-Jan				

Example 1:

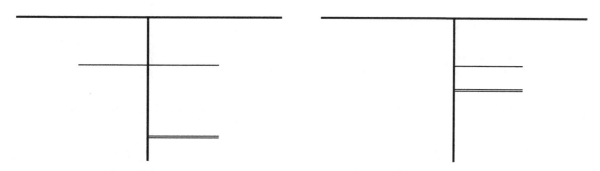

12/31/X1	Unearned Revenues		18,000	
	Revenues			18,000
	To record previously collected revenues now earned			

Example 2:

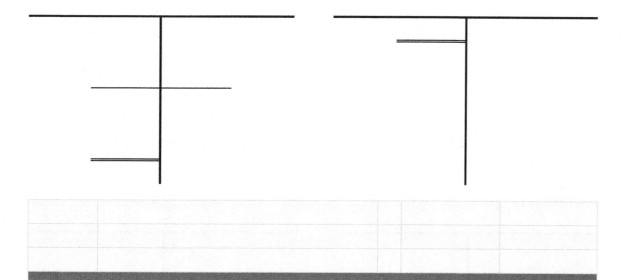

Example 3:

Example 4:

Example 5:

Revenues

Supplies

Rent

Equipment

Wages

Involved Worksheets

Accounting Income vs. Economic Income

Revenues vs. Gains

Expenses vs. Losses

Fiscal Year vs. Calendar Year

Revenue Recognition vs. Expense Recognition

Accruals vs. Prepaids

Balance Sheet Approach vs. Income Statement Approach

Cash Basis vs. Accrual Basis

Record your notes for each team's conclusion on this page:

What is the status of revenue recognition issues, as per the FASB website?

What three companies did your team identify, what are the revenue recognition issues of each, and which is the most interesting?

Record the results of the class wide ranking, noting what factors contribute to complexity of revenue recognition:

GENERAL JOURNAL			
Date	Accounts	Debit	Credit
Dec. 31			
Dec. 31			
Dec. 31			
Dec. 31			
Dec. 31			

GENERAL JOURNAL			Page	
Date	Accounts		Debit	Credit
Mar. 31				
Mar. 31				
Mar. 31				
Mar. 31				
Mar. 31				
Mar. 31				
Mar. 31				

(a)

	Annual Net Income	Assets	Liabilities	Stockholders' Equity
As reported	$5,576,670	$18,942,308	$1,967,638	$16,974,670
Adjustments:				
Accrued expenses	-	-	-	-
Unearned revenues	-	-	-	-
Depreciation	-	-	-	-
Prepaid rent	-	-	-	-
Rebates	-	-	-	-
Correct amounts	$ -	$ -	$ -	$ -

Notes:

    Accrued expenses:

    Unearned revenues:

    Depreciation:

    Prepaid rent:

    Rebates:

(b)

(c)

Scenario 1: Balance Sheet Approach

06/01/X1	Prepaid Insurance		1,500	
	Cash			1,500
	To record payment for 1-year policy			

12/31/X1	Insurance Expense		875	
	Prepaid Insurance			875
	To record insurance "used" ($1,500 X 7/12)			

	Prepaid Insurance			Insurance Expense	
06/01/X1	1,500	875 12/31/X1	12/31/X1	875	
	625				

Scenario 1: Income Statement Approach

06/01/X1	Insurance Expense		1,500	
	Cash			1,500
	To record payment for 1-year policy			

12/31/X1	Prepaid Insurance		625	
	Insurance Expense			625
	To record insurance "unused" ($1,500 X 5/12)			

	Prepaid Insurance			Insurance Expense	
12/31/X1	625		06/01/X1	1,500	625 12/31/X1
				875	

Scenario 2: Balance Sheet Approach

08/01/X1			

12/31/X1			

Unearned Revenue

Revenue

Scenario 2: Income Statement Approach

08/01/X1			

12/31/X1			

Unearned Revenue

Revenue

Scenario 3: Balance Sheet Approach

12/01/X1			

12/31/X1			

Prepaid Rent　　　　　　　　　　Rent Expense

Scenario 3: Income Statement Approach

12/01/X1			

12/31/X1			

Prepaid Rent　　　　　　　　　　Rent Expense

Scenario 4: Balance Sheet Approach

04/01/X1			

06/20/X1			

Unearned Revenue	Revenue

Scenario 4: Income Statement Approach

04/01/X1			

06/20/X1			

Unearned Revenue	Revenue

(a)

WWPS
Cash Basis Income Statement
For the Month Ending June 30, 20XX

Revenues
    Services to customers $ -
Expenses
    Wages $ -
    Equipment   -
    Supplies   -   -
Cash basis income $ -

Cash basis revenues: _____

(b)

WWPS
Income Statement
For the Month Ending June 30, 20XX

Revenues
    Services to customers $ -
Expenses
    Wages $ -
    Depreciation   -
    Supplies   -   -
Net income $ -

Accrual basis revenues: _____

Expenses:

(c)

(d)

(e)

(f)

Chapter 4 Worksheets

Basic Worksheets

(a)

GENERAL JOURNAL				Page	
Date	Accounts			Debit	Credit
Dec. 31					
Dec. 31					
Dec. 31					
Dec. 31					

(b)

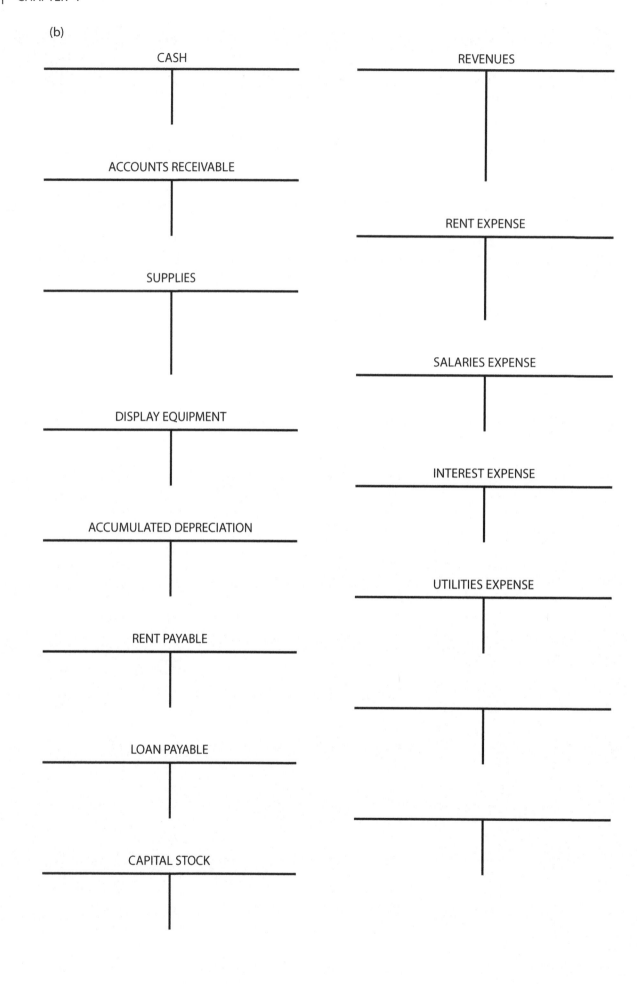

CASH

ACCOUNTS RECEIVABLE

SUPPLIES

DISPLAY EQUIPMENT

ACCUMULATED DEPRECIATION

RENT PAYABLE

LOAN PAYABLE

CAPITAL STOCK

REVENUES

RENT EXPENSE

SALARIES EXPENSE

INTEREST EXPENSE

UTILITIES EXPENSE

(c)

	AMBER NESTOR ART GALLERY Adjusted Trial Balance As of December 31, 20X4	

	Debits	Credits
Cash	$ -	$ -
Accounts receivable	-	-
Supplies	-	-
Display equipment	-	-
Accumulated depreciation	-	-
Rent payable	-	-
Loan payable	-	-
Capital stock	-	-
Revenues	-	-
Rent expense	-	-
Salaries expense	-	-
Interest expense	-	-
Utilities expense	-	-
	-	-
	-	-
	$ -	$ -

Income Statement

Revenues

Services to customers $ -

Expenses

                                                      $ -
                                                                 -
                                                                 -
                                                                 -
                                                                 -                    -
Net income $ -

LAND MONITRIX CORPORATION
Statement of Retained Earnings

Beginning retained earnings $ -

Plus: Net income   -

                                                                         $ -

                                                                                     -

                                                                         $ -

LAND MONITRIX CORPORATION
Balance Sheet

Assets

$ -

-

-

-

Satellite equipment	$	-			
Less: Accumulated depreciation		-		-	
Total assets			$	-	

Liabilities

$ -

-

-

Total liabilities $ -

Stockholders' equity

$ -

-

Total stockholders' equity -

Total liabilities and equity $ -

HIMARIOS COMPANY
Income Statement
For the Year Ending December 31, 20X9

Revenues
  Services to customers $ -

Expenses
                                          $ -
                                                       -
                                                       -
                                          _____   -   _____   -

Net income $ -

HIMARIOS COMPANY
Statement of Retained Earnings
For the Year Ending December 31, 20X9

Beginning retained earnings $ -
Plus: Net income   -
                                                            $ -
Less: Dividends   -
Ending retained earnings $ -

HIMARIOS COMPANY
Balance Sheet
December 31, 20X9

Assets

		$		-
				-
	$	-		-
		-		-
Total assets			$	-

Liabilities

	$	-		
		-		
		-		
		-		
		-		
Total liabilities			$	-

Stockholders' equity

	$	-		
		-		
Total stockholders' equity				-
Total liabilities and equity			$	-

Temporary vs. real accounts

Capital Stock   Real

Revenues   Temporary

Accumulated Depreciation

Salaries Expense

Accounts Payable

Dividends

Supplies

Rent Expense

Unearned Revenues

Income Summary

Equipment

Prepaid Rent

Interest Payable

Retained Earnings

Loan Payable

(a)

GENERAL JOURNAL			Page	
Date	**Accounts**		**Debit**	**Credit**
Dec. 31				
	To close revenues to Income Summary			
Dec. 31				
	To close expenses to Income Summary			
Dec. 31				
	To close Income Summary to retained earnings			
Dec. 31				
	To close dividends			

(b)

CASH	DIVIDENDS
	closing

ACCOUNTS RECEIVABLE	REVENUES
	closing

SUPPLIES	RENT EXPENSE
	closing

EQUIPMENT	SALARIES EXPENSE
	closing

ACCUMULATED DEPRECIATION	SUPPLIES EXPENSE
	closing

ACCOUNTS PAYABLE	INTEREST EXPENSE
	closing

LOAN PAYABLE	DEPRECIATION EXPENSE
	closing

CAPITAL STOCK	INCOME SUMMARY
	closing closing
	closing

RETAINED EARNINGS
closing   closing

(c)

TIMBER CREEK Post-Closing Trial Balance As of December 31, 20X3		
	Debits	**Credits**
	$ -	$ -
	-	-
	-	-
	-	-
	-	-
	-	-
	-	-
	-	-
	-	-
	$ -	$ -

You can either complete this problem by manually redrawing (or cutting and pasting) the shapes, or you can use the Excel file and simply drag and drop the flowchart symbols into the correct sequence.

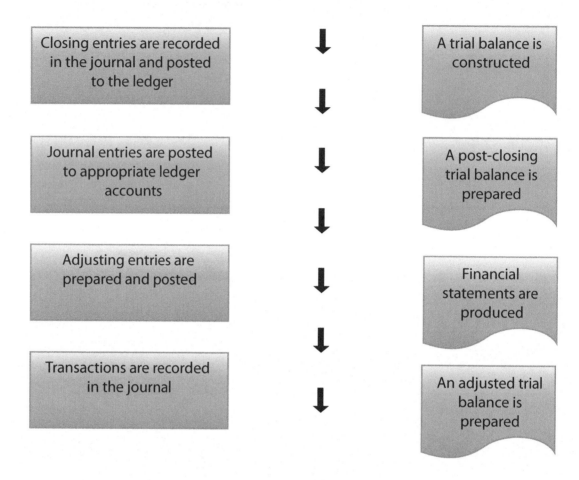

(a)

GENERAL JOURNAL				Page	
Date	Accounts			Debit	Credit
Dec. 31					
Dec. 31					

(b)

(c)

Jan. 1					
Jan. 1					

(d)

Jan. 10					
Jan. 15					

(e)

Jan. 10					
Jan. 15					

(f)

Note: The Excel spreadsheet includes a pick list in column "c," making it easy to select your choice (just click in the applicable cell). The first one is done as an example, and you can select the "blank" item appearing last in the pick list for those accounts that do not appear in the balance sheet.

Note Payable (due in 3 months)   Current Liabilities

Accumulated Depreciation

Investment in Government Bonds

Accounts Receivable

Accounts Payable

Long-term Receivable From Employee

Dividends

Capital Stock

Patent

Supplies

Retained Earnings (ending)

Rent Expense

Unearned Revenues

Income Summary

Equipment

Revenues

Prepaid Rent

Interest Payable

Retained Earnings (beginning)

Loan Payable (due in 5 years)

		Current Assets	Quick Assets	Current Liabilities
Accumulated Depreciation	R 4,569,000			
Prepaid Rent	45,800			
Note Payable (due in 3 months)	100,000			
Accounts Receivable	468,000			
Accounts Payable	255,000			
Patent	3,000,000			
Cash	790,000			
Supplies	134,800			
Unearned Revenues	133,000			
Equipment	8,777,600			
Interest Payable	45,000			
Loan Payable (due in 3 years)	1,500,000			

Working Capital :

Current Ratio:

Quick Ratio:

Involved Worksheets

(a)

GENERAL JOURNAL				Page
Date	**Accounts**		**Debit**	**Credit**

(b)

	BERRY CORPORATION Worksheet for Adjusted Trial Balance December 31, 20X3					
	Trial Balance		Adjustments		Adjusted Trial Balance	
	Debits	Credits	Debits	Credits	Debits	Credits
Cash	$ 30,540		-	-	-	-
Accounts receivable	45,000		-	-	-	-
Supplies	7,000		-	-	-	-
Equipment	244,500		-	-	-	-
Accumulated depreciation	-	$ 46,500	-	-	-	-
Accounts payable	-	12,700	-	-	-	-
Utilities payable	-	-	-	-	-	-
Wages payable	-	-	-	-	-	-
Unearned revenue	-	31,250	-	-	-	-
Notes payable	-	80,000	-	-	-	-
Capital stock	-	100,000	-	-	-	-
Retained earnings, Jan. 1	-	63,200	-	-	-	-
Dividends	12,000	-	-	-	-	-
Revenues	-	289,800	-	-	-	-
Wages expense	214,600	-	-	-	-	-
Utilities expense	8,700	-	-	-	-	-
Selling expense	41,610	-	-	-	-	-
Depreciation expense	12,000	-	-	-	-	-
Supplies expense	-	-	-	-	-	-
Interest expense	7,500	-	-	-	-	-
	$623,450	$623,450	$ -	$ -	$ -	$ -

(c)

BERRY CORPORATION
Income Statement
For the Year Ending December 31, 20X3

Revenues

Services to customers		$ -

Expenses

Wages	$ -	
Utilities	-	
Selling	-	
Depreciation	-	
Supplies	-	
Interest	-	-
Net income		$ -

BERRY CORPORATION
Statement of Retained Earnings
For the Year Ending December 31, 20X3

Beginning retained earnings	$ -
Plus: Net income	-
	$ -
Less: Dividends	-
Ending retained earnings	$ -

BERRY CORPORATION
Balance Sheet
December 31, 20X3

Assets

  Current assets

Cash	$	-		
Accounts receivable		-		
Supplies		-	$	-

  Property, plant, & equipment

Equipment	$	-		
Less: Accumulated depreciation		-		-
Total assets			$	-

Liabilities

  Current liabilities

Accounts payable	$	-		
Utilities payable		-		
Wages payable		-		
Unearned revenue		-	$	-

  Long-term liabilities

Notes payable				-
Total liabilities			$	-

Stockholders' equity

Capital stock	$	-		
Retained earnings		-		
Total stockholders' equity				-
Total liabilities and equity			$	-

(d)

(a)

GENERAL JOURNAL				Page
Date	Accounts		Debit	Credit

(b)

CHESTERFIELD CORPORATION Income Statement For the Year Ending December 31, 20X9		
Revenues		
Services to customers		$ -
Expenses		
Wages	$ -	
Rent	-	
Depreciation	-	
Supplies	-	
Interest	-	-
Net income		$ -

(c)

CHESTERFIELD CORPORATION Statement of Retained Earnings For the Year Ending December 31, 20X9	
Beginning retained earnings	$ -
Plus: Net income	-
	$ -
Less: Dividends	-
Ending retained earnings	$ -

(d)

CHESTERFIELD CORPORATION Balance Sheet December 31, 20X9		
Assets		
Current assets		
Cash	$ -	
Accounts receivable	-	
Supplies	-	
Prepaid rent	-	$ -
Property, plant, & equipment		
Equipment	$ -	
Less: Accumulated depreciation	-	-
Total assets		$ -
Liabilities		
Current liabilities		
Accounts payable	$ -	
Wages payable	-	
Interest payable	-	
Unearned revenue	-	$ -
Long-term liabilities		
Notes payable		-
Total liabilities		$ -
Stockholders' equity		
Capital stock	$ -	
Retained earnings	-	
Total stockholders' equity		-
Total liabilities and equity		$ -

(a)

	WILD RIVER RAFTING CORPORATION WORKSHEET TO PREPARE FINANCIAL STATEMENTS AUGUST 31, 20X5											
	Trial Balance		Adjustments		Adjusted Trial Balance		Income Statement		Statement of Ret. Earnings		Balance Sheet	
	Debit	Credit	Debit	Credit	Debit	Credit	Debit	Credit	Debit	Credit	Debit	Credit

(b)

WILD RIVER RAFTING CORPORATION
Income Statement
For the Year Ending August 31, 20X5

Revenues

$ -

Expenses

$ -

-

-

-

-

-

-        -

Net loss

$ -

WILD RIVER RAFTING CORPORATION
Statement of Retained Earnings
For the Year Ending August 31, 20X5

$ -

-

$ -

-

$ -

WILD RIVER RAFTING CORPORATION
Balance Sheet
August 31, 20X5

Assets

			$	-
	$	-		
		-		-
Total assets			$	-

Liabilities

	$	-		
		-		
		-		
Total liabilities			$	-

Stockholders' equity

	$	-		
		-		
Total stockholders' equity				-
Total liabilities and equity			$	-

(c)

| ITEM #1 | | | | |
Date	Accounts		Debit	Credit
30-Jun	Supplies Expense		10,000	
	Cash			10,000
	Purchased computers with a three-year life and no salvage value			
CORRECTION				

| ITEM #2 | | | | |
Date	Accounts		Debit	Credit
15-Apr	Cash		10,000	
	Revenues			10,000
	Collected customer deposits for future services			
31-Dec	Revenues		2,500	
	Unearned Revenues			2,500
	Completion of 25% of services provided under Apr. 15 agreement			
CORRECTION				

ITEM #3

Date	Accounts		Debit	Credit
30-Sep	Prepaid Insurance		3,000	
	Insurance Expense			3,000
	Purchased for cash a 1-year insurance policy; coverage commences on Oct. 1			

CORRECTION

ITEM #4

Date	Accounts		Debit	Credit
4-Jan	Wages Expense		2,400	
	Cash			2,400
	Paid wages, $1,000 of which was properly accrued at the end of the prior year			

CORRECTION

ITEM #5

Date	Accounts		Debit	Credit
1-Aug	Advertising Expense		9,000	
	Cash			9,000
	Purchased a 9-month advertising campaign from a local newspaper running from Sept. 1 to May 30			
CORRECTION				

ITEM #6

Date	Accounts		Debit	Credit
31-Dec	Utilities Expense		2,500	
	Utilities Payable			250
	Recorded $2,500 of estimated utilities cost for December			
CORRECTION				

The complete accounting cycle I-04.05

(a)

GENERAL JOURNAL				Page 1
Date	Accounts		Debit	Credit

GENERAL JOURNAL — Page 2

Date	Accounts		Debit	Credit

GENERAL JOURNAL — Page 3

Date	Accounts		Debit	Credit

GENERAL JOURNAL			Page 4	
Date	Accounts		Debit	Credit

(b)

Cash

Date	Description	Debit	Credit	Balance
Jan. 1	Balance forward	-	-	-

Accounts Receivable

Date	Description	Debit	Credit	Balance
Jan. 1	Balance forward	-	-	-

Supplies

Date	Description	Debit	Credit	Balance
Jan. 1	Balance forward	-	-	-

Prepaid Insurance

Date	Description	Debit	Credit	Balance
Jan. 1	Balance forward	-	-	-

Equipment

Date	Description	Debit	Credit	Balance
Jan. 1	Balance forward	-	-	-

Accumulated Depreciation

Date	Description	Debit	Credit	Balance
Jan. 1	Balance forward	-	-	-

Accounts Payable

Date	Description	Debit	Credit	Balance
Jan. 1	Balance forward	-	-	-

Interest Payable

Date	Description	Debit	Credit	Balance
Jan. 1	Balance forward	-	-	-

Unearned Revenue

Date	Description	Debit	Credit	Balance
Jan. 1	Balance forward	-	-	-

Notes Payable

Date	Description	Debit	Credit	Balance
Jan. 1	Balance forward	-	-	-

Capital Stock

Date	Description	Debit	Credit	Balance
Jan. 1	Balance forward	-	-	-

Retained Earnings

Date	Description	Debit	Credit	Balance
Jan. 1	Balance forward	-	-	-

Dividends

Date	Description	Debit	Credit	Balance

Revenues

Date	Description	Debit	Credit	Balance

Wage Expense

Date	Description	Debit	Credit	Balance

Fuel Expense

Date	Description	Debit	Credit	Balance

Lodging Expense

Date	Description	Debit	Credit	Balance

Insurance Expense

Date	Description	Debit	Credit	Balance

Supplies Expense

Date	Description	Debit	Credit	Balance

Interest Expense

Date	Description	Debit	Credit	Balance

Depreciation Expense

Date	Description	Debit	Credit	Balance

Income Summary

Date	Description	Debit	Credit	Balance

(c)

FERNANDEZ CORPORATION
Trial Balance
December 31, 20X7

	Debits	Credits
	$ -	$ -
	-	-
	-	-
	-	-
	-	-
	-	-
	-	-
	-	-
	-	-
	-	-
	-	-
	-	-
	-	-
	-	-
	-	-
	$ -	$ -

(d)

GENERAL JOURNAL			Page 5	
Date	Accounts		Debit	Credit

(e)

FERNANDEZ CORPORATION
Adjusted Trial Balance
December 31, 20X7

	Debits	Credits
Cash	$ -	$ -
Accounts receivable	-	-
Supplies	-	-
Prepaid insurance	-	-
Equipment	-	-
Accumulated depreciation	-	-
Accounts payable	-	-
Interest payable	-	-
Unearned revenue	-	-
Notes payable	-	-
Capital stock	-	-
Dividends	-	-
Revenues	-	-
Wage expense	-	-
Fuel expense	-	-
Lodging expense	-	-
Insurance expense	-	-
Supplies expense	-	-
Interest expense	-	-
Depreciation expense	-	-
	$ -	$ -

(f)

FERNANDEZ CORPORATION
Income Statement
For the Year Ending December 31, 20X7

Revenues			
		$	-
Expenses			
	$	-	
		-	
		-	
		-	
		-	
		-	
		-	-
Net income		$	-

FERNANDEZ CORPORATION
Statement of Retained Earnings
For the Year Ending December 31, 20X7

Beginning retained earnings	$	-
Plus: Net income		-
	$	-
Less: Dividends		-
Ending retained earnings	$	-

FERNANDEZ CORPORATION
Balance Sheet
December 31, 20X7

Assets

Current assets

$ -

-

-

-          $ -

Property, plant, & equipment

$ -

-                          -

Total assets $ -

Liabilities

Current liabilities

$ -

-

-          $ -

Long-term liabilities

-

Total liabilities $ -

Stockholders' equity

$ -

-

Total stockholders' equity   -

Total liabilities and equity $ -

(g)

GENERAL JOURNAL				Page 6
Date	Accounts		Debit	Credit

(h)

FERNANDEZ CORPORATION
Post-Closing Trial Balance
December 31, 20X7

	Debits	Credits
	$ -	$ -
	-	-
	-	-
	-	-
	-	-
	-	-
	-	-
	-	-
	-	-
	-	-
	-	-
	-	-
	$ -	$ -

IMAMANI CORPORATION
Balance Sheet
December 31, 20X5

Assets

Liabilities

	FIRST COMPANY	SECOND COMPANY	THIRD COMPANY
Name:			
Working Capital:			
Current Ratio:			
Quick Ratio:			
Commentary:			
Comparison to MD&A comments:			

Chapter 5 Worksheets

Basic Worksheets

Sales, returns and allowances

B-05.01

(a)

GENERAL JOURNAL			Debit	Credit
Date	Accounts			
			350	
				350
	A customer purchased a lighting fixture for cash of €350			
			500	
				500
	A customer purchased a lighting fixture on account for €500			
			275	
				275
	A customer returned a lighting fixture for a cash refund of €275			
			600	
				600
	A customer returned a fixture for a credit on account of €600			
			100	
				100
	A complaining customer received a €100 allowance in cash			
			70	
				70
	A complaining customer received a €70 credit on account			
			475	
				475
	A customer paid their balance on account of €475			

(b)

EURO LIGHTING
Income Statement
For the Year Ending December 31, 20X3

*

* In many European countries, "Sales" is referred to as "Turnover."

(a)

If you elect to solve this problem with the electronic spreadsheet -- all you need to do is enter the number of books in column C and the list price in column D. The rest is automated -- but that is not much of an assignment so I have intentionally included two "errors" in the "If statements" in column H. You will need to identify the errors and correct them to get the right automated answers! Good luck!

	Sale Date	Books	List Price	Trade Discount	Sale Amount	Date Paid	Collection
A	11-Aug			0	$ -	19-Aug	$ -
B	18-Aug			0	-	4-Oct	-
C	3-Sep			0	-	3-Sep	-
D	5-Aug			0	-	20-Sep	-

(b)

A	Accounts Receivable	0.00	
	Sales		0.00
	To record sale to Student A		
	Cash	0.00	
	Sales Discount	0.00	
	Accounts Receivable		0.00
	To record collection from Student A		
B	Accounts Receivable	0.00	
	Sales		0.00
	To record sale to Student B		
	Cash	0.00	
	Sales Discount	0.00	
	Accounts Receivable		0.00
	To record collection from Student B		

(a)

GENERAL JOURNAL				
Date	**Accounts**		**Debit**	**Credit**
5-May				
	Purchased merchandise on account, terms 1/10,n/30			
7-May				
	Returned the Fall Color collection			
10-May				
	Paid invoice, discount taken			
20-May				
	Paid invoice, discount missed			

(b)

GENERAL JOURNAL				
Date	**Accounts**		**Debit**	**Credit**
5-May				
	Purchased merchandise on account, terms 1/10,n/30			
7-May				
	Returned the Fall Color collection			
10-May				
	Paid invoice, discount taken			
20-May				
	Paid invoice, discount missed			

(1)

GENERAL JOURNAL			Debit	Credit
Date	Accounts			
3-Jun				
9-Jun				

(2)

GENERAL JOURNAL			Debit	Credit
Date	Accounts			
7-Jun				
20-Jun				

(3)

GENERAL JOURNAL			Debit	Credit
Date	Accounts			
9-Jun				
20-Jun				

(4)

GENERAL JOURNAL			
Date	Accounts	Debit	Credit
10-Jun			
17-Jun			

(5)

GENERAL JOURNAL			
Date	Accounts	Debit	Credit
12-Jun			
29-Jun			

(6)

GENERAL JOURNAL			
Date	Accounts	Debit	Credit
15-Jun			
27-Jun			

(1)

GENERAL JOURNAL			
Date	**Accounts**	**Debit**	**Credit**
purchase	Purchases	1,000	
	Freight-in	100	
	Accounts Payable		1,100
	F.O.B. Shipping point/freight prepaid		
pay	Accounts Payable	1,100	
	Purchase Discounts		20
	Cash		1,080
	discount taken		

(2)

GENERAL JOURNAL			
Date	**Accounts**	**Debit**	**Credit**
purchase			
	F.O.B. Shipping point/freight prepaid		
pay			
	discount missed		

(3)

GENERAL JOURNAL			
Date	**Accounts**	**Debit**	**Credit**
purchase			
	F.O.B. Destination/freight prepaid		
pay			
	discount taken		

(4)

GENERAL JOURNAL				
Date	Accounts		Debit	Credit
purchase				
	F.O.B. Destination/freight prepaid			
pay				
	discount missed			

(5)

GENERAL JOURNAL				
Date	Accounts		Debit	Credit
purchase				
	F.O.B. Shipping point/freight collect			
pay				
	discount taken			

(6)

GENERAL JOURNAL				
Date	Accounts		Debit	Credit
purchase				
	F.O.B. Shipping point/freight collect			
pay				
	discount missed			

Sales		$ 800,000
Less: Sales discounts	$ 20,000	
Sales returns and allowances	*45,000*	65,000
Net sales		$ 735,000

PITKIN HEALTHCARE PRODUCTS
Income Statement
For the Year Ending December 31, 20X4

GENERAL JOURNAL			Page	
Date	Accounts		Debit	Credit
Dec. 31				
Dec. 31				
Dec. 31				

GENERAL JOURNAL				Page
Date	Accounts		Debit	Credit
purchase				
sale				

MULTIPLE-STEP APPROACH

STOBER'S LAWN SPRINKLER COMPANY
Income Statement
For the Year Ending December 31, 20X7

SINGLE-STEP APPROACH

STOBER'S LAWN SPRINKLER COMPANY
Income Statement
For the Year Ending December 31, 20X7

Morton Corporation

        Sales returns rate:

        Gross profit margin

        Net profit margin

Skyline Corporation

        Sales returns rate:

        Gross profit margin

        Net profit margin

	Morton	Skyline
10% increase in net sales		
Net sales ($926,958 X 110%)		
Cost of goods sold		
Gross profit (net sales X gross profit margin)		
SG&A		
Income before taxes		
Income tax expense (25%)		
Net income		
10% decrease in net sales		
Net sales ($926,958 X 90%)		
Cost of goods sold		
Gross profit (net sales X gross profit margin)		
SG&A		
Income before taxes		
Income tax expense (25%)		
Net income		

The strengths are as follows:

Use this problem as an opportunity to generally consider the benefits of limited access to assets, separation of duties, authorization, use of prenumbered documents, and proper independent verification/audit. Consider how the "other five" suggestions might be ineffective or harmful to the control environment. Be prepared to discuss other ideas (there are many -- e.g., logging the bid price and matching with payments, etc.) for improving controls at the auction.

Involved Worksheets

GENERAL JOURNAL				
Date	**Accounts**		**Debit**	**Credit**
3-Jun				
	Purchased clocks on account, terms 1/10,n/30			
5-Jun				
	Sold clock on account, terms 2/10, n/eom			
9-Jun				
	Paid for the puchase of June 3, taking the 1% discount			
11-Jun				
	Purchased clocks on account, 2/10,n/30, F.O.B. shipping point			
19-Jun				
	Sold clock on account, 2/10, n/eom, F.O.B. destination			
23-Jun				
	Reduced balance due from customer on account of damage			

GENERAL JOURNAL				
Date	**Accounts**		**Debit**	**Credit**
27-Jun				
	Paid the full amount due for the purchase of June 11			
27-Jun				
	Collected the amount due for the sale on June 5			
28-Jun				
	Collected remaining amount for June 19 sale, less 2% discount			

(a)

GENERAL JOURNAL				
Date	**Accounts**		**Debit**	**Credit**
	Purchased cotton for 80,000,000 Pakistan Rupees (PKR), on account			
	Returned cotton for credit on account, PKR 3,000,000			
	Agreed with suppliers to purchase price allowances, PKR 5,000,000			
	Made payment on PKR 60,000,000 of open accounts within discount period, and received PKR 600,000 purchase discounts			
	Made payment on PKR 12,000,000 of open accounts outside of discount period, and lost PKR 120,000 purchase discounts			

(b)

GENERAL JOURNAL				
Date	**Accounts**		**Debit**	**Credit**
	Purchased cotton for 80,000,000 Pakistan Rupees (PKR), on account			
	Returned cotton for credit on account, PKR 3,000,000			
	Agreed with suppliers to purchase price allowances, PKR 5,000,000			
	Made payment on PKR 60,000,000 of open accounts within discount period, and received PKR 600,000 purchase discounts			
	Made payment on PKR 12,000,000 of open accounts outside of discount period, and lost PKR 120,000 purchase discounts			

(c)

CTC Income Statement For the Month Ending June 30, 20XX (all amounts in thousands of PKR)	
Revenues	
Net sales	97,000
Cost of goods sold	
Gross profit	
Expenses	
Net income	

(d)

CTC
Income Statement
For the Month Ending June 30, 20XX
(all amounts in thousands of PKR)

Revenues

   Net sales   97,000

Cost of goods sold

Gross profit

Expenses

Net income

(a)

HANNA SPORTS CORPORATION Income Statement For the Year Ending December 31, 20X7

Revenues

Cost of goods sold

Gross profit

Expenses

Net income

(b)

GENERAL JOURNAL				Page
Date	Accounts		Debit	Credit
Dec. 31				
	To close income statement accounts with a credit balance, and establish ending inventory balance			
Dec. 31				
	To close income statement accounts with a debit balance, and remove the beginning inventory balance			
Dec. 31				
	To close Income Summary to Retained Earnings			
Dec. 31				
	To close Dividends to Retained Earnings			

(a)

GENERAL JOURNAL				
Date	**Accounts**		**Debit**	**Credit**
T#1				
	Periodic -- recording of purchase (assuming gross method)			
	vs.			
	Periodic -- recording of purchase (assuming net method)			
	vs.			
	Perpetual -- recording of purchase (assuming gross method)			
	vs.			
	Perpetual -- recording of purchase (assuming net method)			

GENERAL JOURNAL				
Date	Accounts		Debit	Credit
T#2				
	Periodic -- recording of payment (assuming gross method)			
	vs.			
	Periodic -- recording of payment (assuming net method)			
	vs.			
	Perpetual -- recording of payment (assuming gross method)			
	vs.			
	Perpetual -- recording of payment (assuming net method)			

GENERAL JOURNAL				
Date	Accounts		Debit	Credit
T#3				
	Periodic -- recording of sale (assuming gross method)			
	vs.			
	Periodic -- recording of sale (assuming net method)			
	vs.			
	<u>and</u>			
	Perpetual -- recording of sale (assuming gross method)			
	vs.			
	<u>and</u>			
	Perpetual -- recording of sale (assuming net method)			

(b)

With the perpetual system, the general ledger tracks the cost of goods sold on an ongoing basis. The account contains _____.

Further, the Inventory account contains _____.

With the gross periodic system, the calculation of cost of goods sold would be as follows:

Beginning inventory

Plus: Net purchases

Cost of goods available for sale

Less: Ending inventory *

Cost of goods sold

With the net periodic system, the calculation of cost of goods sold would be as follows:

Beginning inventory

Plus: Purchases

Cost of goods available for sale

Less: Ending inventory *

Cost of goods sold

* Ending inventory would be determined by a physical count (this presentation assumes it would "match" amounts found in the perpetual system ledger).

MONTAQUE CORPORATION
Income Statement
For the Year Ending December 31, 20X5
(all amounts in thousands of dollars)

Revenues

Sales			$5,675,000
Less: Sales discounts		$ -	
Sales returns and allowances		-	-
Net sales			$ -

Cost of goods sold

Beginning inventory, Jan. 1		$ -	
Add: Purchases	$ -		
Freight-in	-		
	$ -		
Less: Purchase discounts	$ -		
Purchase returns & allowances	-	-	
Net purchases		-	
Goods available for sale		$ -	
Less: Ending inventory, Dec. 31		-	
Cost of goods sold			-

Gross profit $ -

Selling expenses

Advertising	$ -		
Salaries	-		
Depreciation	-		
Utilities	-	$ -	

General & administrative expenses

Salaries	$ -		
Depreciation	-		
Utilities	-	-	

Other expenses

Interest		-	-

Income before taxes $ -

Income tax expense   -

Net income $ -

This solution is reached by setting up the format, inserting the knowns, and solving for the unknowns. The excel version includes formulas that reveal the logic of each number.

MONTAQUE CORPORATION
Income Statement
For the Year Ending December 31, 20X5
(all amounts in thousands of dollars)

Revenues

Net sales $ -

Expenses

Cost of goods sold	$ -	
Selling	-	
General & administrative expenses	-	
Interest	-	-

Income before taxes $ -

Income tax expense -

Net income $ -

This problem will have many different solutions and approaches. No worksheet is provided.

Basic Worksheets

Composition of cash	**B-06.01**

(a) Currency in the petty cash box

Cash

(b) Postage stamps in a file cabinet

(c) The balance on deposit in a regular checking account

(d) An advance to an employee for travel costs to be incurred

(e) A certificate of deposit maturing in 2 years

(f) A 30-day certificate of deposit

(g) An investment in a government treasury security maturing in 2 years

(h) A 90-day government treasury security

(i) A post-dated check accepted from a customer

(j) Amounts due from customers

(k) Amounts paid to suppliers by check, but the supplier has not yet cashed the check

Borrowing money

May result in risk of financial failure

Attempting to accelerate customer collections

Delaying payments

Writing checks against future receipts not yet deposited

Slowing expansion plans

Establishing bank overdraft protection or a line of credit

Issuing additional capital stock

Planning full utilization of cash flows, with no reserves

Ending balance per bank statement		$144,223.99
Add:		
		-
Deduct:		
		-
Correct cash balance		$ -

Ending balance per company records			$ 72,644.12
Add:			
	$ -		
	-		-
Deduct:			
	$ -		
	-	-	
Correct cash balance			$ -

GENERAL JOURNAL				
Date	**Accounts**		**Debit**	**Credit**
	To record adjustments necessitated by bank reconciliation			

GENERAL JOURNAL			Debit	Credit
Date	**Accounts**		**Debit**	**Credit**
#1				
	To establish a $500 petty cash fund			
#2				
	To record expenses and replenishment of petty cash			
#3				
	To record expenses and replenishment/increase to petty cash			

GENERAL JOURNAL				
Date	**Accounts**		**Debit**	**Credit**
7-May				
	To record the purchase of 500,000 shares of Kuai stock at $7 per share			
31-May				
	To record a $_____ per share increase in the value of 500,000 shares of Kuai stock			
30-Jun				
	To record a $_____ per share decrease in the value of 500,000 shares of Kuai stock			
15-Jul				
	To record a $0.10 per share cash dividend on the investment in Kuai stock			
31-Jul				
	To record a $_____ per share increase in the value of 500,000 shares of Kuai stock			

Involved Worksheets

Cash composition and management	I-06.01

The company has a 1-year certificate of deposit, and it is earning 5% interest. The bank has offered to swap this CD for a 1-month CD bearing a 4.5% interest rate.

The company holds significant investments in "trading" securities. These investments have typically yielded about 8% per year. The company can sell these securities and convert the proceeds to cash.

The company carries several million dollars of accounts payable, terms 2/10, n/30. The company always takes the discount, but can delay payment to preserve cash.

The company can begin to offer cash discounts of 1/10, n/30 on its receivables, and anticipates that this would greatly speed cash collections.

The company maintains a significant investment in postage stamps and travel advances. The company can buy postage "as needed" via an internet linked postage meter, and the company can do away with travel advances and provide key employees with a company credit card to use for travel costs.

The company is considering establishing a line of credit that enables it to borrow, on demand, up to $5,000,000 in cash. The bank will charge a $12,500 annual fee for making this credit line available to the company. Any borrowed funds will accrue interest at the established London Interbank Offered Rate (LIBOR) plus 1%.

(a)

Ending balance per bank statement		$288,090.09
Add:		
		-
Deduct:		
	$ -	
	-	
	-	
	-	
	-	-
Correct cash balance		$ -

Ending balance per company records		$ -
Add:		
	$ -	
	-	-
Deduct:		
	$ -	
	-	
	-	
	-	-
Correct cash balance		$ -

(b) The corect Cash balance is

(c)

GENERAL JOURNAL				
Date	**Accounts**		**Debit**	**Credit**
	To record adjustments necessitated by bank reconciliation			

Ending balance per bank statement		$	-
Add:			
			-
Deduct:			
	$	-	
		-	
		-	-
Correct cash balance		$	-

Ending balance per company records		$	-
Add:			
	$	-	
		-	
		-	-
Deduct:			
	$	-	
		-	
		-	
		-	-
Correct cash balance		$	-

GENERAL JOURNAL			Debit	Credit
Date	Accounts			
	To record adjustments necessitated by bank reconciliation			

This problem provides a tangible, team exercise pertaining to the correct operation of a petty cash fund. Begin by forming a nine-person team consisting of four employees, a banker, a petty cash custodian, a treasurer, an accountant, and an auditor.

Step 1

The treasurer will prepare a check to create a $100 petty cash fund, and present this check to the banker who will cash the check. The accountant should record this transaction in the journal.

Step 2

The treasurer will present the cash to the petty cash custodian, and each employee will next present his or her receipts for reimbursement. You may assume presented receipts are legitimate and meet company guidelines.

Step 3

Employee #1, who has not been reimbursed by the fund for any expenses, will reconcile the petty cash account in the presence of the petty cash custodian. The employee will inform the treasurer of the amount needed for reimbursement. The treasurer will prepare a check for reimbursement and to increase the total petty cash fund to a balance of $150. The treasurer will present the check to the bank and provide the funds to the petty cash custodian. The accountant should record this activity in the journal.

EMPLOYEE # 1   Your objective is to be sure that receipts plus cash equal the $100 fund amount. You should observe the petty cash custodian perform the count. It would be a bad practice for you to actually touch the money since you would then be a "suspect" in any shortage that might exist. Prepare a memo detailing the results of your review of petty cash. Be sure to include a listing of the expenses incurred by the fund and a statement confirming the remaining cash balance. Present this memo to the treasurer and the accountant.

EMPLOYEE # 2   Clip this receipt and present it to the petty cash custodian for reimbursement. The customer agreed to reimburse Centennial for the overnight delivery cost, so make a prominent notation on the receipt for the accounting department to be sure and bill the customer.

Overnight Parcel Express

Shipment # 579709587
Jan. 15, 20X5

Sender	Centennial Corp.
	4648 Westover Rd.
Recipient	Broadway Industries
	789 Fairway Lane #120
Contents	Overnight package - electronic parts
Delivery	Guaranteed by 10 a.m. - recipent signature req'd
Amount	$45.00
Payment	Cash received from customer

EMPLOYEE # 3   Present the following receipt to the petty cash custodian for reimbursement. This meal was with Arnold Zavier, a key customer. Your meeting with Arnold was to discuss a new product line. Tax rules require that you document the purpose of the meal and the involved persons. Make an appropriate notation directly on the receipt and attach your signature. (Note: As an aside, tax laws place limitations on the deductibility of such costs in determining a company's tax liability.)

Szechuan Restaurant
Fine food with fun!
Jan. 20, 20X5

Lunch special (2 @ $8.75)	$17.50
Iced tea	1.75
Hot tea	1.50
	$20.75
Tax	1.60
Total	$22.35
Tip	3.65
Total Ticket	$26.00

Thank you for dining with us!
May good fortune come your way today!

EMPLOYEE # 4   Present the following receipt to the petty cash custodian for reimbursement. This fuel was to "top off" the tank on a company vehicle prior to sending it out on a lengthy road trip.

RUN TIME PETROLEUM
8487 Northwest Highway

Jan. 25, 20X5

Unleaded regular gasoline	(3 gallons @ $4)	$ 12.00
	Total	$ 12.00

BANKER   Use the following "currency" and pay the checks presented by the treasurer. Be sure the checks are made payable to "cash" and not "petty cash." The treasuer should sign the check on the front and endorse the check on the back.

$20 TWENTY DOLLARS	$10 TEN DOLLARS	$5 FIVE DOLLARS
$20 TWENTY DOLLARS	$10 TEN DOLLARS	$5 FIVE DOLLARS
$20 TWENTY DOLLARS	$10 TEN DOLLARS	$5 FIVE DOLLARS
$20 TWENTY DOLLARS	$10 TEN DOLLARS	$5 FIVE DOLLARS
$20 TWENTY DOLLARS	$10 TEN DOLLARS	$5 FIVE DOLLARS
$20 TWENTY DOLLARS	$10 TEN DOLLARS	$1 ONE DOLLAR
$20 TWENTY DOLLARS	$10 TEN DOLLARS	$1 ONE DOLLAR
$20 TWENTY DOLLARS	$10 TEN DOLLARS	$1 ONE DOLLAR
$20 TWENTY DOLLARS	$10 TEN DOLLARS	$1 ONE DOLLAR
$20 TWENTY DOLLARS	$10 TEN DOLLARS	$1 ONE DOLLAR

PETTY CASH
CUSTODIAN
Accept the cash provided by the treasurer and reimburse receipts presented by employees. Custodians should maintain a record of activities that includes signatures from employees who receive reimbursement or place funds into the account. Use the following form for this purpose. It is also a good practice to be sure that each receipt is clearly marked with the purpose of the expenditure and to whom reimbursement is made. Mark each receipt as "paid" at the time of reimbursement.

Date	Item	Amount	Signature

TREASURER
Properly complete the checks and present them to the banker for cashing. Provide the funds to the custodian. It is a good practice to have the custodian sign a "receipt" acknowledging that he or she has accepted the funds.

Centennial Corp.
4648 Westover Rd.

Check #

Date: _____

Pay to the order of: _____ $ _____

DOLLARS

♦ *Meridian Bank* ♦

MEMO _____   _____

Centennial Corp.
4648 Westover Rd.

Check #

Date: _____

Pay to the order of: _____ $ _____

DOLLARS

♦ *Meridian Bank* ♦

MEMO _____   _____

I acknowledge receipt of _____ dollars from _____

for the purpose of establishing or replenishing the petty cash fund over which I am custodian.

Date: _____   Signed: _____

I acknowledge receipt of _____ dollars from _____

for the purpose of establishing or replenishing the petty cash fund over which I am custodian.

Date: _____   Signed: _____

AUDITOR   At the conclusion of this problem, review the procedures and documentation used by your team and identify if there were any errors or irregularities. Do you have any suggestions for improving controls?

Lead your team in a discussion of the importance of a good accounting system. For instance, how would Centennial insure that the shipping costs get billed back to Broadway, how would costs that have unique tax treatment (like the meal) be tracked and documented, and so forth. Focus the discussion on the importance of proper accounting systems and controls as a necessity in correctly managing business resources.

ACCOUNTANT   Record the check to establish the petty cash fund.

Concurrent with the treasurer's reimbursement of the fund, obtain the receipts from the custodian along with a copy of the report prepared by Employee #1. Examine the documents for any discrepancies and prepare an appropriate journal entry.

GENERAL JOURNAL

Date	Accounts		Debit	Credit
	To establish petty cash fund			
	To replenish and increase petty cash fund			

GENERAL JOURNAL				
Date	Accounts		Debit	Credit
1-Aug				
31-Aug				
30-Sep				
31-Oct				

GENERAL JOURNAL				
Date	Accounts		Debit	Credit
Day 1				
	To record the purchase of short-term investments			
Day 1				
	To record increase/decrease in value of short-term investments			
Day 2				
	To record increase/decrease in value of short-term investments			
Day 3				
	To record increase/decrease in value of short-term investments			
Day 4				
	To record increase/decrease in value of short-term investments			
Day 5				
	To record increase/decrease in value of short-term investments			

Basic Worksheets

	Cash Only		*Direct Extension of Credit*		*Accept Credit Cards*	
	Advantage	Disadvantage	Advantage	Disadvantage	Advantage	Disadvantage
Opportunity to charge/collect additional income in the form of interest		✓	✓			✓
Likely increase in revenues						
Conducting credit background check/ obtaining a credit report						
Significant risk of uncollectible accounts						
Increased accounting cost in the form of periodic billings						
Incurrence of fees on each transaction						
Immediate access to proceeds						

GENERAL JOURNAL				
Date	**Accounts**		**Debit**	**Credit**
11-Jun				
	Sold merchandise on "bank card;" same day funding, net of fee of 1.5% assessed by bank			
11-Jun				
	Sold merchandise on "nonbank card," recorded 4% fee			
25-Jun				
	Collected amount due from credit card company			

The direct write off method

B-07.03

(a)

(b)

(c)

GENERAL JOURNAL				
Date	Accounts		Debit	Credit
Dec. 31				

(d)

(a)

(b)

GENERAL JOURNAL				
Date	Accounts		Debit	Credit
various				
	To record the write off of uncollectible accounts			

(c)

GENERAL JOURNAL				
Date	Accounts		Debit	Credit
Dec. 31				
	To adjust the allowance account from a $18,000 balance to the target balance of _____			

(d)

Accounts receivable

Less: Allowance for Uncollectible Accounts

(e)

(a)

Spreadsheet						▢▢✖
			fx			
	A	B	C	D	E	F
1	Age	Balance	Estimated % Uncollectible	Estimated Amount Uncollectible		
2	0 to 30 days					
3	31 to 60 days					
4	61 to 120 days					
5	Over 120 days					
6						
7						

Accounts receivable

Less: Allowance for uncollectibles

(b)

GENERAL JOURNAL				
Date	Accounts		Debit	Credit
Dec. 31				

(c)

GENERAL JOURNAL				
Date	Accounts		Debit	Credit
Dec. 31				

Critical thinking about account balances

(a)

GENERAL JOURNAL				
Date	Accounts		Debit	Credit
Jan. 31				
	To record January sales			
Jan. 31				
	To establish the uncollectible accounts expense for January			
Jan. 31				
	To write-off accounts deemed uncollectible			
Jan. 31				
	To record cash colletctions			

GENERAL JOURNAL				
Date	Accounts		Debit	Credit
Feb. 28				
	To record February sales			
Feb. 28				
	To establish the uncollectible accounts expense for February			
Feb. 28				
	To write-off accounts deemed uncollectible			
Feb. 28				
	To record cash colletctions			

GENERAL JOURNAL				
Date	**Accounts**		**Debit**	**Credit**
Mar. 31				
	To record March sales			
Mar. 31				
	To establish the uncollectible accounts expense for March			
Mar. 31				
	To write-off accounts deemed uncollectible			
Mar. 31				
	To record cash colletctions			

(b)

(c)

(a), (c)

GENERAL JOURNAL				
Date	Accounts		Debit	Credit

(b)

(a)

Accounts Receivable Turnover Ratio
=

.

Days Outstanding
=

(b)

(c)

(1) Payee

(2) Principal

(3) Dishonor

(4) Maker

(5) Interest

(6) Maturity

Vinay missed _____ questions and _____ eligible for the job. Correct Vinay's paper below:

(a)

Assume the bank holds a 400,000 Indian Rupee (INR) note receivable dated June 1, 20X1. This note matures on August 31, 20X1. This note is written to assume a 360 day year and 30 day months. The annual interest rate is stated at 10%. What is the maturity value of the note, including interest?

Answer: 400,000 X 10% X 60/360 = 6,666.67

400,000 + 6,666.67 = <u>406,666.67</u>

(b)

Assume the bank holds a INR 400,000 note receivable dated June 1, 20X1. This note matures on August 31, 20X1. This note is written to assume a 365 day year, and actual days outstanding are used in all calculations. The annual interest rate is stated at 10%. What is the maturity value of the note, including interest?

Answer: 400,000 X 10% X 92/365 = <u>10,082.19</u>

(c)

Assume the bank holds a INR 1,000,000 note receivable dated October 1, 20X5. This note matures on September 30, 20X6. This note is written to assume a 360 day year and 30 day months. The annual interest rate is stated at 8%. How much interest income should the bank record for its accounting year ending December 31, 20X5?

Answer: Zero, the note is not due until 20X6

(d)

Assume the bank holds a INR 1,000,000 note receivable dated October 1, 20X5. This note matures on September 30, 20X6. This note is written to assume a 360 day year and 30 day months. The annual interest rate is stated at 8%. How much interest income should the bank record for its accounting year ending December 31, 20X6?

Answer: 1,000,000 X 8% X 270/360 = <u>600,000</u>

GENERAL JOURNAL				
Date	**Accounts**		**Debit**	**Credit**
Dec. 1				
	To record issuance of 10%, 1-year note, in exchange for outstanding receivable			
Dec. 31				
	To accrued interest on note ($24,000 X 10% X 1/12)			
Nov. 30				
	To record interest income (11 months) and collection of note receivable and previously accrued interest			

Involved Worksheets

Direct write-off versus allowance methods	I-07.01

(a)

GENERAL JOURNAL				
Date	**Accounts**		**Debit**	**Credit**
Year 1	No Entry			
Year 2				
Year 3				

(b)

(c)

GENERAL JOURNAL			
Date	Accounts	Debit	Credit
Year 1			
Year 2			
Year 2			
Year 3			
Year 3			

(d)

(a)

GENERAL JOURNAL				
Date	**Accounts**		**Debit**	**Credit**
	To record sales on account			
	To record collections on account			
	To record sales discounts			
	To write-off uncollectible accounts			
	To increase allowance			

(b)

GENERAL JOURNAL				
Date	**Accounts**		**Debit**	**Credit**
	To record sales on account			
	To record collections on account			
	To record sales discounts			
	To write-off uncollectible accounts			
	To increase allowance (see calculations on next page)			

	Receivables		Allowance	
Beginning balance (20X7)	$ 1,500,000		$ 40,000	
Sales on account (20X7)	-		-	
Collections on account (20X7)	-		-	
Sales discounts (20X7)	-		-	
Accounts written off (20X7)	-		-	
Additions to allowance (20X7)	-		-	
Ending balance (20X7)	$ -		$ -	

	Receivables		Allowance	
Beginning balance (20X8)	$ -		$ -	
Sales on account (20X8)	-		-	
Collections on account (20X8)	-		-	
Sales discounts (20X8)	-		-	
Accounts written off (20X8)	-		-	
Subtotals	$ -		$ -	
* Additions to allowance (20X8)	-		-	
Ending balance (20X8)	$ -		$ -	

*

(c)

(a)

GENERAL JOURNAL				
Date	**Accounts**		**Debit**	**Credit**
	To record the write-off of the Windy Point receivable			
	To restore the portion of the Windy Point receivable that was collected			
	To record the collection of the Windy Point receivable			
	To record sales on account			
	To record collections on account			
	To record the write-off of accounts			
	To establish the correct balance in the allowance			

(b)

	ACCOUNTS RECEIVABLE	ALLOWANCE FOR UNCOLLECTIBLES	NET REALIZABLE VALUE	UNCOLLECTIBLE ACCOUNTS EXPENSE
To record the write-off of the Windy Point receivable	$ (150,000)	$ (150,000)	$ -	$ -
To restore the portion of the Windy Point receivable that was collected				
To record the collection of the Windy Point receivable				
To record sales on account				
To record collections on account				
To record the write-off of accounts				
To establish the correct balance in the allowance for uncollectibles				

(a)

Customer	Date of Sale	Amount
Air There Freight	December 11, 2019	12,300
Aurora	November 12, 2019	5,000
Batesville	August 18, 2019	14,805
CarMan	December 9, 2019	21,900
Clinic Quick	August 15, 2018	16,040
Delorres River Guides	September 19, 2019	8,990
Elonzo's Restaurant	December 17, 2019	11,789
Hospital Supply	December 4, 2019	135,100
Inidigo	November 29, 2019	16,500
Meridan Oil	May 20, 2019	11,786
Museum of Art	December 21, 2019	255,000
Novellus	February 16, 2019	18,780
Norman's	December 23, 2019	10,000
Robert Ricketts	December 14, 2019	3,550
Sanchez Systems	October 25, 2019	22,310
Security by the Hour	December 13, 2019	40,900
Stop Shop	December 27, 2019	34,700
Target Time	February 3, 2019	14,440
Uvlade Ranch	December 7, 2019	3,700
Xhi	October 20, 2019	15,100
Zebra Sports	December 3, 2019	144,000

Spreadsheet						▭▢✕
			fx			
	A	B	C	D	E	F
1	Age	Balance	Estimated % Uncollectible	Estimated Amount Uncollectible		
2	0 to 30 days		1%	$ -		
3	31 to 90 days		3%	-		
4	91 to 180 days		10%	-		
5	Over 180 days		40%	-		
6				$ -		
7						

(b)

GENERAL JOURNAL				
Date	Accounts		Debit	Credit

(c)

GENERAL JOURNAL				
Date	Accounts		Debit	Credit

(d)

Each group is anticipated to have unique solutions based on the companies selected.

(a) - (d)

GENERAL JOURNAL				
Date	Accounts		Debit	Credit
(a)				
(b)				
(c)				
(d)				

(e)

(f)

Basic Worksheets

	Inventory		Category		
	Yes	No	Raw Material	Work in Process	Finished Goods
Finished stretch limos awaiting sale	✓				✓
Limos under production that have been ordered by specific customers and a deposit made					
Finished limos shipped to dealers, terms FOB shipping point					
Luxury cars ordered from a manufacturer and in transit, FOB destination					
Sheet metal in the company's warehouse					
Wiring produced in China, in transit on a ship in the Pacific Ocean, terms FOB Shanghai					
Leather installed on a limo currently under production					
LCD monitors installed in a finished limo awaiting shipment to a customer					
Finished and sold limo returned to the factory for repair under warranty					

(a)

The art gallery is the _____ and the artists are the _____. The inventory should be carried on the balance sheets of the _____.

(b)

The items for inclusion in inventory are to be selected from the list below:

See Shining Sea	Gallery	$2,500
Mermaids	Artist	1,800
Big Fish	Gallery	910
Shells At Dawn	Gallery	3,000
Sand Forever	Gallery	1,090
Development!	Artist	4,200
Taking a Chance	Gallery	20,000
Tides and Moons	Gallery	500
Mystery Sea	Gallery	1,200
On the Beach	Artist	1,650
Too Much Sun	Artist	4,775
Spring Break	Artist	5,000
Inland	Gallery	7,880
Alligators Return	Artist	19,720
Frost and Farm	Gallery	14,300

TOTAL OWNED INVENTORY AT RETAIL $ -

DIVIDED BY MARKUP RATE

TOTAL INVENTORY VALUE FOR THE BALANCE SHEET $ -

(c)

GENERAL JOURNAL			
Date	Accounts	Debit	Credit
	To record sale of art held on consignment		

Basic inventory cost flow concepts   B-08.03

(a)

(b)

(c)

(d)

(e)

(f)

(g)

(a)

FIFO

Beginning inventory	$	-
Plus: Purchases		-
Cost of goods available for sale	$	-
Less: Ending inventory		-
Cost of goods sold	$	-

Sales	$	-
Cost of goods sold		-
Gross profit	$	-

(b)

LIFO

Beginning inventory	$	-
Plus: Purchases		-
Cost of goods available for sale	$	-
Less: Ending inventory		-
Cost of goods sold	$	-

Sales	$	-
Cost of goods sold		-
Gross profit	$	-

(c)

Weighted-average

Beginning inventory	$	-
Plus: Purchases		-
Cost of goods available for sale	$	-
Less: Ending inventory		-
Cost of goods sold	$	-

Sales	$	-
Cost of goods sold		-
Gross profit	$	-

FIFO perpetual:

Date	Purchases	Cost of Goods Sold	Balance
Day 0			10 X $10 = $100
Day 1			
	5 X $11 = $55		
Day 2			
Day 3			
	8 X $12 = $96		
Day 4			
Ending			

LIFO perpetual:

Date	Purchases	Cost of Goods Sold	Balance
Day 0			10 X $10 = $100
Day 1			
	5 X $11 = $55		
Day 2			
Day 3			
	8 X $12 = $96		
Day 4			
Ending			

Moving average:

Date	Purchases	Cost of Goods Sold	Balance
Day 0			10 X $10 = $100
Day 1			
	5 X $11 = $55		
Day 2			
Day 3			
	8 X $12 = $96		
Day 4			
Ending			

(a)

GENERAL JOURNAL				
Date	Accounts		Debit	Credit

(b)

(c)

GENERAL JOURNAL				
Date	Accounts		Debit	Credit

(d)

UNITS SOLD

UNITS IN ENDING INVENTORY

Sales

Cost of goods sold

Gross profit

Lower of cost or net realizable value   *B-08.08*

(a)

	Fire	Horse	Baby	War	Rain	Election
COST						
Vs. "NRV":						
Expected selling price						
Selling expense						
Net realizable value						
VALUE TO REPORT						

(b)

(c)

(d)

Gross profit estimation technique

	A	B	C	D	E
1					
2	Sales*				
3	Cost of goods sold				
4	Gross profit				
5					
6	* Sales = $48,000/.06 =				
7					
8	Beginning Inventory				
9	Plus: Purchases				
10	Cost of goods available for sale				
11	Less: Ending inventory before theft				
12	Cost of goods sold				
13					

The cost to retail percentage is _____.

The following analysis shows that sales of _____ were matched with cost of sales of _____. This results in gross profit of _____.

	A	B	C	D	E
Spreadsheet					
	A	B	C	D	E
1		At Cost (___% of Retail)		At Retail	
2	Beginning Inventory	$ 46,800		$ 78,000	
3	Purchases*	230,000		-	
4	Cost of goods available for sale	$ -		$ -	
5	Sales	-		-	
6	Ending Inventory**	$ -		$100,000	
7					

* Purchases at retail =

** Ending inventory at cost =

(a)

(b)

20X2 Inventory Turnover Ratio
=

20X3 Inventory Turnover Ratio
=

(a)

	20X7		20X8	
Beginning inventory	$ -		$ -	
Purchases	-		-	
Cost of goods available for sale	$ -		$ -	
Less: Ending inventory	-		-	
Cost of goods sold	$ -		$ -	
Sales	$ -		$ -	
Cost of goods sold	-		-	
Gross profit	$ -		$ -	

(b)

	20X7		20X8	
Beginning inventory	$ -		$ -	
Purchases	-		-	
Cost of goods available for sale	$ -		$ -	
Less: Ending inventory	-		-	
Cost of goods sold	$ -		$ -	
Sales	$ -		$ -	
Cost of goods sold	-		-	
Gross profit	$ -		$ -	

(c)

(d)

Involved Worksheets

QUESTION   Are "finished goods" synonymous with "cost of goods sold?"

ANSWER

QUESTION   How does the negotiation of freight terms impact total inventory?

ANSWER

QUESTION   Are consigned goods included in inventory?

ANSWER

QUESTION   Is "inventory" also called "cost of goods available for sale"?

ANSWER

QUESTION   How does LIFO result in cash savings during a period of rising prices?

ANSWER

QUESTION   Will a periodic and perpetual system give me the same results?

ANSWER

QUESTION   It seems like the "gross profit" method is much simpler than FIFO, LIFO, or average costing.
            Can I use it as my primary inventory valuation technique?

ANSWER

QUESTION   How can I use the retail inventory technique to estimate inventory theft?

ANSWER

QUESTION   What's the big deal if I undercount ending inventory? The goods are still there so there is
            no real problem, right?

ANSWER

(a)

FIFO

Purchases

50 units @ $15,000 each

70 units @ $16,000 each

30 units @ $16,500 each

90 units @ $17,000 each

25 units @ $17,200 each

Beginning inventory	$	-
Plus: Purchases		-
Cost of goods available for sale	$	-
Less: Ending inventory		-
Cost of goods sold	$	-
Sales	$	-
Cost of goods sold		-
Gross profit	$	-

(b)

LIFO

Beginning inventory	$	-
Plus: Purchases		-
Cost of goods available for sale	$	-
Less: Ending inventory		-
Cost of goods sold	$	-
Sales	$	-
Cost of goods sold		-
Gross profit	$	-

(c)
Weighted-average

Beginning inventory	$	-
Plus: Purchases		-
Cost of goods available for sale	$	-
Less: Ending inventory		-
Cost of goods sold	$	-

Sales	$	-
Cost of goods sold		-
Gross profit	$	-

(d)

The highest gross profit is produced under _____.

The most current cost in inventory is reported under _____.

The most current cost on the income statement is reported under _____.

The lowest profit and tax obligation is produced under _____.

(a) FIFO perpetual:

Date	Purchases	Sales	Cost of Goods Sold	Balance
1-Jan				5,000 X $20 = $100,000
5-Jan	7,000 X $21 = $147,000			
12-Jan		9,000 @ $35 = $315,000		
17-Jan	4,000 X $22 = $ 88,000			
26-Jan		3,000 @ $37 = $111,000		
31-Jan				

(b) Moving average:

Date	Purchases	Sales	Cost of Goods Sold	Balance
1-Jan				5,000 X $20 = $100,000
5-Jan	7,000 X $21 = $147,000			
12-Jan		9,000 @ $35 = $315,000		
17-Jan	4,000 X $22 = $ 88,000			
26-Jan		3,000 @ $37 = $111,000		
31-Jan				

(c)

GENERAL JOURNAL			Debit	Credit
Date	**Accounts**			
7-Jan				
	Purchased $147,000 of inventory on account (7,000 X $21)			
12-Jan				
	Sold merchandise on account (9,000 X $35)			
12-Jan				
	To record the cost of merchandise sold			
17-Jan				
	Purchased $88,000 of inventory on account (4,000 X $22)			
26-Jan				
	Sold merchandise on account (3,000 X $37)			
26-Jan				
	To record the cost of merchandise sold			

(d)

(e)

(f)

(a)

First Team Member -- Assuming FIFO, identify if the lender conditions are anticipated to be met.

	Purchases	Available for Sale	Cost of Goods Sold	Ending Inventory
		$ -	$ -	$ -
		-	-	-
		-	-	-
		-	-	-
		-	-	
			$ -	$ -

Gross Profit Rate

Sales (16,000 X $5,000)	$ -
Cost of goods sold	-
Gross profit	$ -

Inventory Turnover

Cost of goods sold	$ -
÷ Ending inventory (substituted for average inventory)	÷ -
Turnover rate	

Current Ratio

Current assets	$ -
÷ Current liabilities	÷ -
Current ratio	

(b)

<u>Second Team Member</u> -- Obtain the first team member's results. If all lender conditions were not met, determine if a change in planned 4th quarter purchases would allow all conditions to be met.

Purchases	Available for Sale	Cost of Goods Sold	Ending Inventory
	$ -	$ -	$ -
	-	-	-
	-	-	-
	-	-	-
	-	-	-
		$ -	$ -

<u>Gross Profit Rate</u>

Sales (16,000 X $5,000)	$ -
Cost of goods sold	-
Gross profit	$ -

<u>Inventory Turnover</u>

Cost of goods sold	$ -
÷ Ending inventory (substituted for average inventory)	÷ -
Turnover rate	

<u>Current Ratio</u>

Current assets	$ -
÷ Current liabilities	÷ -
Current ratio	

(c)

<u>Third Team Member</u> -- Assuming LIFO, identify if the lender conditions are anticipated to be met.

	Purchases	Available for Sale	Cost of Goods Sold	Ending Inventory
		$ -	$ -	$ -
		-	-	-
		-	-	-
		-	-	-
		-		-
			$ -	$ -

<u>Gross Profit Rate</u>

Sales (16,000 X $5,000)		$ -
Cost of goods sold		-
Gross profit		$ -

<u>Inventory Turnover</u>

Cost of goods sold		$ -
÷ Ending inventory (substituted for average inventory)		÷ -
Turnover rate		

<u>Current Ratio</u>

Current assets		$ -
÷ Current liabilities		÷ -
Current ratio		

(d)

<u>Fourth Team Member</u> -- Obtain the third team member's results. If all lender conditions were not met, determine if a change in planned 4th quarter purchases would allow all conditions to be met.

	Purchases	Available for Sale	Cost of Goods Sold	Ending Inventory
		$ -	$ -	$ -
		-	-	-
		-	-	-
		-	-	-
		-	-	-
			$ -	$ -

<u>Gross Profit Rate</u>

Sales (16,000 X $5,000)	$ -
Cost of goods sold	-
Gross profit	$ -

<u>Inventory Turnover</u>

Cost of goods sold	$ -
÷ Ending inventory (substituted for average inventory)	÷ -
Turnover rate	

<u>Current Ratio</u>

Current assets	$ -
÷ Current liabilities	÷ -
Current ratio	

(e)

Fifth Team Member -- Assuming the weighted-average inventory method, identify if the lender conditions are anticipated to be met.

	Purchases	Available for Sale
		$ -
		-
		-
		-
		$ -

Gross Profit Rate

Sales (16,000 X $5,000)	$ -
Cost of goods sold	-
Gross profit	$ -

Inventory Turnover

Cost of goods sold	$ -
÷ Ending inventory (substituted for average inventory)	÷ -
Turnover rate	

Current Ratio

Current assets	$ -
÷ Current liabilities	÷ -
Current ratio	

(f)

Sixth Team Member -- Obtain the fifth team member's results. If all lender conditions were not met, determine if a change in planned 4th quarter purchases would allow all conditions to be met.

Purchases	Available for Sale	
	$	-
		-
		-
		-
		-
	$	-

Gross Profit Rate

Sales (16,000 X $5,000)	$	-
Cost of goods sold		-
Gross profit	$	-

Inventory Turnover

Cost of goods sold	$	-
÷ Ending inventory (substituted for average inventory)	÷	-
Turnover rate		

Current Ratio

Current assets	$	-
÷ Current liabilities	÷	-
Current ratio		

(g)

The various errors are analyzed below.

A spreadsheet of beginning inventory included 35 Zing golf bags at a cost of $20 each. These particular bags were the nicest in the store, and the unit cost was actually $200. The error was the result of incorrect data entry into the spreadsheet.

The ending inventory value was the result of a physical count on December 31, 20X8. The count failed to include 2,400 imprinted logo golf balls that were in the custody of employees who were going to be giving them away as promotional items at a New Year's Day parade on January 1, 20X9. These balls cost $1.50 each.

The company experienced a theft loss during 20X8. The theft consisted of 6 sets of Caldaway golf clubs that normally sell for $1,000 each, and provide a gross profit margin of 45%. The insurance company purchased replacement goods and delivered them to Southwest Golf Shop. These club sets were included in the year end physical inventory and valued at $1,000 each.

In 20X8, the company consigned golf apparel with a retail value of $30,000 to a vendor at a local golf tournament. The cost to retail percentage on apparel is 60%. At the conclusion of the tournament, the vendor returned $12,000 (at retail) of goods and $18,000 in cash. The agreement was that Southwest Golf Shop would pay the vendor a commission equal to 15% of the gross profit margin on sales. The commission has not yet been calculated or paid.

At year end, the company had 10 units of the Big Face driver in stock. The drivers had a unit cost of $300 and were included in the year end inventory at $3,000 total. The manufacturer of Big Face has just announced a new driver, the Square Face. These units will render the Big Face mostly obsolete. Even though the manufacturer will continue to offer Big Face for sale at a dealer cost of $300, it is anticipated the customers will now be willing to pay no more than $200 retail for the item.

REVISED DATA:

Sales	$	-
Cost of goods sold		-
Gross profit		-
Operating expenses		-
Income before tax		-
Ending inventory	$	-
Beginning inventory		-

Basic Worksheets

	Type	Basic Accounting
Debt Investments:		
Investment in debt with a plan to hold until a particular future event of payoff		
Investment in debt with the goal of a near-term profit		
Investments in debt other than one of the above two types		
Equity Investments:		
Investment in equity generally over 20% but not giving control		
Investment in equity usually over 50%		
Relatively permanent investments in equity other than one of the above two types		

The ~~Securities and Exchange Commission~~ Financial Accounting Standards Board is increasingly issuing standards focused on fair value accounting.

Potential questions (anticipated answer):

(a)

(b)

GENERAL JOURNAL				
Date	Accounts		Debit	Credit
5-Aug				
31-Aug				
30-Sep				
15-Oct				
31-Oct				

(a)(b)(c)

GENERAL JOURNAL				
Date	**Accounts**		**Debit**	**Credit**
Issue				
Interest				
Maturity				

(d)

(a)(b)(c)

GENERAL JOURNAL				
Date	Accounts		Debit	Credit
Issue				
Interest				
Maturity				

(d)

(a)(b)(c)

GENERAL JOURNAL				
Date	Accounts		Debit	Credit
Issue				
Interest				
Maturity				

(d)

(a)

(b)

GENERAL JOURNAL				
Date	Accounts		Debit	Credit

(c)

Basic consolidated balance sheet

Consolidating Spreadsheet			
A	B	C	D
Accounts	Packed Powder	Snowfall	Consolidated
2 Cash	$ 450,000	$ 60,000	$ -
3 Accounts receivable	400,000	185,000	-
4 Inventory	1,250,000	125,000	-
5 Investment in Snowfall	2,000,000	-	-
6 Land	850,000	380,000	-
7 Buildings and equipment (net)	1,300,000	1,700,000	-
8	$6,250,000	$2,450,000	$ -
9			
10 Accounts payable	$ 760,000	$ 150,000	$ -
11 Notes payable	2,400,000	300,000	-
12 Common stock	500,000	400,000	-
13 Retained earnings	2,590,000	1,600,000	-
14	$6,250,000	$2,450,000	$ -

Goodwill in a consolidated balance sheet

Consolidating Spreadsheet			
A	B	C	D
Accounts	Parrot	Sparrow	Consolidated
2 Cash	$1,450,000	$ 160,000	$ -
3 Accounts receivable	430,000	335,000	-
4 Inventory	850,000	725,000	-
5 Investment in Sparrow	5,000,000	-	-
6 Land	550,000	500,000	-
7 Buildings and equipment (net)	1,700,000	2,530,000	-
8 * Goodwill	-	-	-
9	$9,980,000	$4,250,000	$ -
10			
11 Accounts payable	$ 460,000	$ 450,000	$ -
12 Notes payable	1,700,000	800,000	-
13 Common stock	2,530,000	1,000,000	-
14 Retained earnings	5,290,000	2,000,000	-
15	$9,980,000	$4,250,000	$ -

Involved Worksheets

(a)

GENERAL JOURNAL				
Date	**Accounts**		**Debit**	**Credit**
Invest				
Dividend				
Income				
Price				

(b)

GENERAL JOURNAL				
Date	Accounts		Debit	Credit
Invest				
Interest				
Income				
Price				

(c)

GENERAL JOURNAL				
Date	Accounts		Debit	Credit
Invest				
Dividend				
Income				
Price				

(a)

	A	B	C	D	E	F	G
				fx			
1	Date		Cash Received		Interest Income		Investment in Bonds
2	1-1-X1		$ -				$ -
3	6-30-X1		-		$ -		-
4	12-31-X1		-		-		-
5	6-30-X2		-		-		-
6	12-31-X2		-		-		-
7	6-30-X3		-		-		-
8	12-31-X3		-		-		-
9	6-30-X4		-		-		-
10	12-31-X4		-		-		-
11	6-30-X5		-		-		-
12	12-31-X5		-		-		-
13	6-30-X6		-		-		-
14	12-31-X6		-		-		-
15	12-31-X6		-		-		-
16			$ -		$ -		
17							

(b)

	A	B	C	D	E	F	G	H	I
	Spreadsheet								
				fx					
1	Date		Cash Received		Interest Income		Discount Amortization		Investment in Bonds
2	1-1-X1		$ -						$ -
3	6-30-X1		-		$ -		$ -		-
4	12-31-X1		-		-		-		-
5	6-30-X2		-		-		-		-
6	12-31-X2		-		-		-		-
7	6-30-X3		-		-		-		-
8	12-31-X3		-		-		-		-
9	6-30-X4		-		-		-		-
10	12-31-X4		-		-		-		-
11	6-30-X5		-		-		-		-
12	12-31-X5		-		-		-		-
13	6-30-X6		-		-		-		-
14	12-31-X6		-		-		-		-
15	12-31-X6		-		-		-		-
16			$ -		$ -		$ -		
17									

(c)

	A	B	C	D	E	F	G	H	I
							Premium Amortization		**Investment in Bonds**
1	Date		Cash Received		Interest Income				
2	1-1-X1		$ -						$ -
3	6-30-X1		-		$ -		$ -		-
4	12-31-X1		-		-		-		-
5	6-30-X2		-		-		-		-
6	12-31-X2		-		-		-		-
7	6-30-X3		-		-		-		-
8	12-31-X3		-		-		-		-
9	6-30-X4		-		-		-		-
10	12-31-X4		-		-		-		-
11	6-30-X5		-		-		-		-
12	12-31-X5		-		-		-		-
13	6-30-X6		-		-		-		-
14	12-31-X6		-		-		-		-
15	12-31-X6		-		-		-		-
16			$ -		$ -		$ -		
17									

(d)

(a)

GENERAL JOURNAL				
Date	Accounts		Debit	Credit
Issue				
Interest				
Maturity				

(b)

GENERAL JOURNAL				
Date	Accounts		Debit	Credit
Issue				
Interest				
Maturity				

(c)

GENERAL JOURNAL				
Date	Accounts		Debit	Credit
Issue				
Interest				
Maturity				

(a)

GENERAL JOURNAL				
Date	Accounts		Debit	Credit

(b)

PRINCETON CORPORATION AND CONSOLIDATED SUBSIDIARY
Balance Sheet
July 1, 20X5

Assets

Current assets

Cash	$ -		
Accounts receivable	-		
Inventories	-	$ -	

Property, plant, & equipment

Land	$ -		
Building (net of accumulated depreciation)	-		
Equipment (net of accumulated depreciation)	-	-	

Intangible assets

Goodwill	$ -		
Patent	-	-	
Total assets		$ -	

Liabilities

Current liabilities

Accounts payable	$ -		
Salaries payable	-	$ -	

Long-term liabilities

Loan payable		-	
Total liabilities		$ -	

Stockholders' equity

Capital stock	$ -		
Retained earnings	-		
Total stockholders' equity		-	
Total liabilities and equity		$ -	

The investment in Alpha:

GENERAL JOURNAL				
Date	**Accounts**		**Debit**	**Credit**

The investment in Beta:

GENERAL JOURNAL				
Date	**Accounts**		**Debit**	**Credit**

The investment in Delta:

GENERAL JOURNAL				
Date	**Accounts**		**Debit**	**Credit**

The investment in Gamma:

GENERAL JOURNAL				
Date	**Accounts**		**Debit**	**Credit**

Basic Worksheets

Balance sheet presentation of property, plant, and equipment	*B-10.01*

Property, Plant & Equipment

The sign cost is computed as follows:

GENERAL JOURNAL				
Date	Accounts		Debit	Credit

	Capital		Category			
	Yes	No	Land	Land Improvement	Building	Equipment
Delivery cost of new furniture	✔					✔
Wages paid to guard at office building						
Fees for title insurance on land purchase						
Cost of periodic repainting of parking lot						
Cost of building new sidewalks						
Interest costs on loan to buy equipment						
Computer training class on general commercial software package						
Interest cost on loan during construction period for new building						
Architects fees for new building						
Installation and setup costs on new machinery						
Repair of damage to device broken during initial installation						
Safety violation fines at construction site						
Tap fees for connecting new building to city water system						

GENERAL JOURNAL				
Date	**Accounts**		**Debit**	**Credit**

	Operating Lease	Financing Lease
The lessee reports the leased asset on its balance sheet		✓
Payments are reported fully as rent expense		
Ownership of the property passes to the lessee by the end of the lease term		
The lease term exceeds one year		
Interest expense is measured and reported by the lessee		
Depreciation of the leased asset is not reported by the lessee		
At the inception of the lease, the lessee records both an asset and liability		
The lessee reports a liability for the present value of all future payments anticipated under the lease agreement		
The lessor continues to report the tangible asset covered by the lease on its balance sheet		

(a)

Year	Annual Expense	Accumulated Depreciation at End of Year	Annual Expense Calculation
X3			
X4			
X5			
X6			
X7			

(b)

Property, Plant & Equipment (20X5)

Equipment

Less: Accumulated depreciation

(c)

GENERAL JOURNAL				
Date	Accounts		Debit	Credit
1-Jan				
	To record the purchase of press			
31-Dec 20X3				
	To record 20X3 depreciation			
31-Dec 20X4				
	To record 20X4 depreciation			
31-Dec 20X5				
	To record 20X5 depreciation			
31-Dec 20X6				
	To record 20X6 depreciation			
31-Dec 20X7				
	To record 20X7 depreciation			
31-Dec 20X7				
	To record disposal of asset			

(a)

Year	Annual Expense	Accumulated Depreciation at End of Year	Annual Expense Calculation
X6			
X7			
X8			
X9			

(b)

Property, Plant & Equipment (20X7)

Aircraft engine

Less: Accumulated depreciation

(c)

GENERAL JOURNAL			
Date	**Accounts**	**Debit**	**Credit**
1-Jan			
	To record the purchase of engine		
31-Dec			
20X6			
	To record 20X6 depreciation		
31-Dec			
20X7			
	To record 20X7 depreciation		
31-Dec			
20X8			
	To record 20X8 depreciation		
31-Dec			
20X9			
	To record 20X9 depreciation		
31-Dec			
20X9			
	To record disposal of asset		

(a)

Year	Annual Expense	Accumulated Depreciation at End of Year	Annual Expense Calculation
X1			
X2			
X3			
X4			

(b)

Property, Plant & Equipment (20X3)

Equipment

Less: Accumulated depreciation

(c)

GENERAL JOURNAL				
Date	Accounts		Debit	Credit
1-Jan				
	To record purchase of excavator			
31-Dec 20X1				
	To record 20X1 depreciation			
31-Dec 20X2				
	To record 20X2 depreciation			
31-Dec 20X3				
	To record 20X3 depreciation			
31-Dec 20X4				
	To record 20X4 depreciation			
31-Dec 20X4				
	To record disposal of asset			

Year	Annual Expense	Accumulated Depreciation at End of Year	Annual Expense Calculation
X1			
X2			
X3			
X4			
X5			
X6			
X7			
X8			

Involved Worksheets

1 Cost minus salvage value
  Depreciable base

2 Cost minus accumulated depreciation

3 Depreciation is a process of this, rather than valuation

4 Costs that are added to an asset account

5 Costs of items added to a land-related account, like paving and landscaping

6 A bundled purchase of assets

7 Lessee does not report the asset

8 Like straight-line, but the denominator is not time

9 A tax-based allocation of cost that is not GAAP

10 Justification for expensing small items

11 Included with land cost

12 Expensed immediately

13 Results in less depreciation each year than the year before

	Land	Land Improvement	Building	Equipment	Expense
Item 1					$2,500
Item 2					
Item 3					
Item 4					
Item 5					
Item 6					
Item 7					
Item 8					
Item 9					
Item 10					
Totals					

A correcting journal entry would include the following:

(a) Straight-line

Year	Annual Expense	Accumulated Depreciation at End of Year	Annual Expense Calculation
X2			
X3			
X4			
X5			
X6			

(b) Units of Output

Year	Annual Expense	Accumulated Depreciation at End of Year	Annual Expense Calculation
X2			
X3			
X4			
X5			
X6			

(c) Double-declining balance

Year	Annual Expense	Accumulated Depreciation at End of Year	Annual Expense Calculation
X2			
X3			
X4			
X5			
X6			

(d) Straight-line revised

Year	Annual Expense	Accumulated Depreciation at End of Year	Annual Expense Calculation
X2			
X3			
X4			
X5			
X6			
X7			

<u>Building:</u>

<u>Truck:</u>

Results:

```



```

Straight line result

```



```

Double-declining result

Formulas:

```



```

Straight line result

```



```

Double-declining result

Team-based analysis of depreciation methods used

Complete the following table for your team:

COMPANY	USEFUL LIVES			METHOD(s)
	Buildings	Equipment	Other	

Basic Worksheets

	Classification:		For Capital Items:	
	Capital	Revenue	Replacement	Betterment
Routine cleaning and repainting		✓		
Replacement of expensive cables and pulleys				
Addition of directional drilling motor				
Safety inspection fee				
Raising and lowering rig at each new drill site				
Interest cost on loan to buy rig				
Installation of additional advanced lighting system technology				
Turntable, deck, and bearings in place of similar worn out unit				
Lubrication of all moving parts				
Welding broken outrigger mount				
Installation of anti-slip flooring on all smooth surface walk ways				

GENERAL JOURNAL				
Date	Accounts		Debit	Credit
	To record addition to existing building			
	To record addition of landscaping			
	To record replacement of siding material			
	To record replacement of light bulbs			

GENERAL JOURNAL				
Date	**Accounts**		**Debit**	**Credit**
Case 1				
Case 2				
Case 3				

GENERAL JOURNAL				
Date	**Accounts**		**Debit**	**Credit**
Tractor A				
Tractor B				

	Impaired?	
	Yes	No
An abandoned building is slated for demolition	✓	
Equipment that will continue to be used as planned in the production of profitable projects; however, a forced sale of the equipment would not recover its book value		
Used equipment is no longer in use, but will be sold for more than its book value		
Newly purchased assets for which the company significantly overpaid, and which have costs that will not be recovered from future cash flows		
Actions of competitors have forced McMahan to permanently lower prices, and certain items of equipment continue to be used at full capacity, even though the resulting production is unprofitable and will not recover cost		
The maintenance department failed to properly lubricate the bearings on a crane, and it is now significantly damaged		

GENERAL JOURNAL				
Date	**Accounts**		**Debit**	**Credit**
Year 3				
	To record depletion of oil well			

GENERAL JOURNAL				
Date	**Accounts**		**Debit**	**Credit**

Involved Worksheets

GENERAL JOURNAL				
Date	Accounts		Debit	Credit

<u>Item A</u>

<u>Item B</u>

<u>Item C</u>

<u>Item D</u>

GENERAL JOURNAL				
Date	Accounts		Debit	Credit
	To record sale of Asset A			
	To record sale of Asset B			
	To record sale of Asset C			
	To record sale of Asset D			

(a)   Largest gain

(b)   Largest loss

(c)   Highest depreciation to avoid

(d)   Largest immediate cash flow

(e)   Largest addition to total assets

(f)   No change in assets

GENERAL JOURNAL				
Date	**Accounts**		**Debit**	**Credit**

GENERAL JOURNAL				
Date	Accounts		Debit	Credit

Preliminary depletion calculation:

Depreciation calculations:

      Digging equipment:

      Hauling equipment:

Annual income calculations:

	Revenues	Labor and Operating	Depreciation	Depletion	Annual Income
Year 1					
Year 2					
Year 3					
Year 4					
Year 5					
Year 6					
Year 7					
Year 8					
Year 9					
Year 10					

(a)

(b)

(c)

GENERAL JOURNAL

Date	Accounts		Debit	Credit

Summary statement from Student A:

Summary statement from Student B:

Summary statement from Student C:

Summary statement from Student D:

Basic Worksheets

	Condition:	Other Conditions to meet:
A	Obligation is due within one year	C, D, or E
B	Obligation is due within the operating cycle	
C	Obligation requires the use of current assets	
D	Obligation results in the creation of another current liability	
E	Obligation to be satisfied by providing services	

Liabilities

  Current liabilities

	$	-		
		-		
		-		
		-		
		-		
		-	$	-

Supporting calculations:

(a), (b), (c)

GENERAL JOURNAL				
Date	Accounts		Debit	Credit

(a), (b), (c)

GENERAL JOURNAL				
Date	**Accounts**		**Debit**	**Credit**
1-Apr				
31-Dec				
31-Mar				

(d)

Make necessary corrections below in red:

The first loan was a one-year loan for $100,000, created on November 1 of the current year. It bears interest at 8%, with interest based on the "rule of 78s."

Calculations:

$$\$100,000 \ X \ 8\% \ X \ 2/12 = \$1,333.33$$

The second loan is due on demand and was for $250,000. The loan was originated on November 1 of the current year, and it bears interest at 9%, using a 360-day year assumption.

Calculations:

$$\$250,000 \ X \ 9\% \ X \ 2/12 = \$3,750.00$$

The financial statement implications of the above corrections are:

(a)

(b)

(c)

GENERAL JOURNAL				
Date	Accounts		Debit	Credit

(a)

| BAYLOR HEALTH | | Check # | 95859 |
| Payroll Account | | Date: | June 30, 20XX |

Pay to the order of: _____

_____

First Corner Bank

MEMO   June payroll for Bodine   *Judy Baylor*

Detach below before depositing, and save for your records.

Employee: L. Bodine	Gross Earnings		$	-
Pay period: June 20XX	**Deductions:**			
	Federal Income Tax	$ -		
	Social Security Tax	-		
	Medicare/Medicaid Tax	-		
	Insurance	-		
	Retirement Savings Plan	-		
	Charity	-		
	Net Pay		$	-

Supporting calculations:

(b)

GENERAL JOURNAL				
Date	Accounts		Debit	Credit

(c)

Each of Wilson's comments was wrong. Following is an evaluation of the incorrect statements:

Wilson
"The company is a fraud! It has a defined contribution plan for its employees and does not list the pension assets and liabilities on its books! Sell, sell, sell!"

Correction

Wilson
"You have to love this company. They are very conservative. They even accrue a liability for health insurance coverage relating to future retirees. Nobody does that! This company's real earnings are much higher than they are letting on. Buy, buy, buy!"

Correction

Wilson
"Well, it's true that peoples' feet are growing larger, so maybe this a good play. But, beware because the company is not accruing costs related to employee sick leave. They offer some lame excuse about not meeting all four criteria of an applicable accounting rule. Wrong, you only need to meet one of the criteria! Sell, sell, sell!"

Correction

Wilson
"Buy! The company offers employees a defined benefit pension plan. The pension trust is loaded with loot, yet the company continues to show a pension liability on its books. It's a hidden asset."

Correction

Involved Worksheets

Recording and reporting for typical current liabilities   *I-12.01*

(a)

GENERAL JOURNAL				
Date	**Accounts**		**Debit**	**Credit**

(b)

GENERAL JOURNAL				
Date	Accounts		Debit	Credit

(c)

Liabilities

Current liabilities

$ -

          -

          -

          -

          -

          -

          -     $ -

(a)

GENERAL JOURNAL				
Date	Accounts		Debit	Credit

(b)

GENERAL JOURNAL				
Date	Accounts		Debit	Credit

The company is subject to several lawsuits by plaintiffs. These claims assert that the camouflage is so effective that opposing paintballers come into too close of a range, and are therefore hurt by high-velocity, close-up shots. The company's attorney views the likelihood of any adverse judgment as highly remote. Further, the company generally has seen increased sales because of publicity associated with these claims.

The company manufactures a face shield that has been prone to crack. As a result, several serious injuries have been reported. The company is generally willing to settle each documented claim for $20,000. Currently, it is estimate that 45 such claims will be submitted and settled.

The company has issued a full product recall of the defective face shields, and expects to spend $700,000 on issuing replacement shields. The new shields will not be distributed until the next fiscal year.

The company has been notified by a competitor that one of Camo Max's camouflage designs violates a copyright held by the competitor. The competitor is asking for a $250,000 paid up license to the use the design. Camo Max disagrees, but believes that it is reasonably possible the competitor will fill a copyright infringement action.

Subsequent to year end (but before preparing financial statements), an employee was seriously injured by a fabric cutting machine. The company has agreed to a large financial settlement with the employee. This payment will eliminate any hope of profitability during the next several years.

(a)

| Name | Gross Earnings | Deductions | | | | | Net Earnings |
		Federal Income Tax	Social Security Tax	Medicare/ Medicaid	Charitable	Health Insurance	
Breschi, K							
Carballo, P							
Dangelo, J							
Gaines, T							
Goseco, M							
Skolnick, J							
Williams, R							
Wong, O							
Totals	$ -	$ -	$ -	$ -	$ -	$ -	$ -

(b)

GENERAL JOURNAL				
Date	**Accounts**		**Debit**	**Credit**
31-Oct				
	To record payroll			
31-Oct				
	To record employer portion of payroll taxes and benefits			

Complete the following table for each company identified by your team. Be sure to note whether the company reports any balance sheet asset or liability related to its plans, or any other points of interest:

COMPANY	Pension Plans		Other Post Retirement Benefits?
	Defined Benefit?	Defined Contribution?	

Basic Worksheets

Basic accounting for long-term note payable   *B-13.01*

(a), (b), (c), (d), (e)

GENERAL JOURNAL				
Date	**Accounts**		**Debit**	**Credit**
04-01-X4				
12-31-X4				
03-31-X5				
12-31-X5				
03-31-X6				

(a)   7% interest, and 6 periods:

(b)   7% interest, and 6 periods:

The future value factor from the table is

(c)

Year of Investment	Future Value Factor From Table	Payment	Value of Payment at end of 6th Year
1 (amount will be invested 6 years)		$10,000	$ -
2 (amount will be invested 5 years)		$10,000	-
3 (amount will be invested 4 years)		$10,000	-
4 (amount will be invested 3 years)		$10,000	-
5 (amount will be invested 2 years)		$10,000	-
6 (amount will be invested 1 year)		$10,000	-
			$ -

(d)   7% interest, and 6 periods:

The future value factor from the annuity table is

Present value concepts

(a)   6% interest, and 4 periods:

(b)   6% interest, and 4 periods:

The present value factor from the table is

(c)

Year	Present Value Factor From Table	Payment	Value of Payment at beginning of 1st Year
1 (amount will be received in 1 year)		$25,000	$ -
2 (amount will be received in 2 years)		$25,000	-
3 (amount will be received in 3 years)		$25,000	-
4 (amount will be received in 4 years)		$25,000	-
			$ -

(d)   6% interest, and 4 periods:

The present value factor from the annuity table is

(a)

Loan Amount = Payments X Annuity Present Value Factor

(b)

GENERAL JOURNAL				
Date	**Accounts**		**Debit**	**Credit**
1-Jan	Building		500,000.00	
	Note Payable			500,000.00
	To record purchase of office building for 9% note payable			
31-Dec	Interest Expense			
	Note Payable			
	Cash			
	To record payment			
31-Dec	Interest Expense			
	Note Payable			
	Cash			
	To record payment			

(c)

Loan Amount = Payments X Annuity Present Value Factor

The specific terms of a bond issue are specified in a bond debenture. Secured bonds are backed up only by the general faith and credit of the issuer. Computerization has resulted in the virtual elimination of registered bonds. Serial bonds must be matched with funds set aside in a fund to provide for the eventual retirement of the issue. Callable bonds can be exchanged for common stock of the issuer. Low-yield bonds of distressed firms are frequently called junk bonds. Bonds will sell at a premium when the effective rate is above the stated rate.

(a), (b), (c)

GENERAL JOURNAL				
Date	Accounts		Debit	Credit
Issue				
Interest				
Maturity				

(d)

(a), (b), (c)

GENERAL JOURNAL			
Date	Accounts	Debit	Credit
Issue			
Interest			
Maturity			

(d)

(a), (b), (c)

GENERAL JOURNAL				
Date	**Accounts**		**Debit**	**Credit**
Issue				
Interest				
Maturity				

(d)

Bonds at a premium, effective-interest amortization *B-13.09*

(a)

(b)

GENERAL JOURNAL				
Date	**Accounts**		**Debit**	**Credit**
1-Jan				
30-Jun				
31-Dec				

(c)

Bonds payable $ -

Plus: Premium on bonds payable - $ -

(a)

(b)

GENERAL JOURNAL				
Date	Accounts		Debit	Credit
1-Jan				
30-Jun				
31-Dec				

(c)

Bonds payable	$ -	
Less: Discount on bonds payable	-	$ -

(a), (b), (c)

GENERAL JOURNAL				
Date	Accounts		Debit	Credit
1-Mar				
30-Jun				
31-Dec				

GENERAL JOURNAL				
Date	Accounts		Debit	Credit
31-Dec				
31-Dec				

(a)

Total Assets	Total Liabilities	Total Debt/ Total Assets
_____	_____	_____

(b)

Total Assets	Total Liabilities	Total Equity (Assets - Liabilities)	Total Debt/ Total Equity
_____	_____	_____	_____

(c)

Net Income	Income Before Tax (Net income/ 70%)	Interest Expense (Total Liabilities X 8%)	Income Before Tax and Interest	Income Before Interest and Tax/ Interest
_____	_____	_____	_____	_____

(d)

Commitments and leases

(a), (b), (c), (d)

GENERAL JOURNAL				
Date	Accounts		Debit	Credit
(a)				
(b)				
(c)				
(d)				

(e)

Involved Worksheets

(a)

How much will a lump sum of $10,000, invested at 7% per annum, grow to in 20 years?

(b)

How much will be in account after 2 years, if $50 is placed into the account at the beginning of each month? Assume the account's interest rate is 6%, with monthly compounding.

(c)

How much should be set aside today, so that it will grow to $30,000 in 15 years? The discount rate is 9%.

(d)

What is the present worth of an income stream that includes annual end-of-period payments of $100,000 for 20 years? Assume the appropriate discount rate is 8% per year.

(a)

GENERAL JOURNAL				
Date	Accounts		Debit	Credit
1-Apr 20X3				
31-Dec 20X3				
31-Mar 20X4				
31-Dec 20X4				
31-Mar 20X5				

(b)

(c)

GENERAL JOURNAL				
Date	Accounts		Debit	Credit
1-Apr 20X5				
30-Jun 20X5				
30-Sep 20X5				

(d)

Period	Beginning Balance	Interest (Beginning Balance X 1.5%)	Amount of Payment	Principal Reduction (payment minus interest)	Ending Balance
1	$1,200,000.00	$18,000.00	$69,894.88	$51,894.88	$1,148,105.12
2	1,148,105.12				
3					
4					
5					
6					
7					
8					
9					
10					
11					
12					
13					
14					
15					
16					
17					
18					
19					
20					

(a)

Period Ending	Beginning of Period Net Book Value of Bonds Payable	Interest Expense (Net Book Value X 5% X 6/12)	Amount of Payment	Premium Amortization (payment minus expense)	End of Period Net Book Value (beginning balance less amortization)
6-30-X2	$2,102,578				
12-31-X2					
6-30-X3					
12-31-X3					
6-30-X4					
12-31-X4					
6-30-X5					
12-31-X5					
6-30-X6					
12-31-X6					
6-30-X7					
12-31-X7					

(b)

GENERAL JOURNAL			
Date	Accounts	Debit	Credit
1-Jan			
30-Jun			
31-Dec			

(c)

Bonds payable	$	-
Plus: Unamortized premium on bonds payable	-	$	-

Bonds issued at a discount; effective interest   *I-13.04*

(a)

Period Ending	Beginning of Period Net Book Value of Bonds Payable	Interest Expense (Net Book Value X 7% X 6/12)	Amount of Payment	Discount Amortization (expense minus payment)	End of Period Net Book Value (beginning balance plus amortization)
6-30-X3	$4,792,085				
12-31-X3					
6-30-X4					
12-31-X4					
6-30-X5					
12-31-X5					
6-30-X6					
12-31-X6					
6-30-X7					
12-31-X7					

(b)

GENERAL JOURNAL			
Date	Accounts	Debit	Credit
1-Jan			
30-Jun			
31-Dec			

(c)

Bonds payable	$ -	
Less: Unamortized discount on bonds payable	-	$ -

Each team member will have unique calculations.

Periodic interest payments ($100,000 X ?%)	$ -	
Present value factor (10-period annuity, ?%)	X _____ -	$ -
Maturity value	$ 100,000	
Present value factor (10 periods, ?%)	X _____ -	$_____ -
Price of bonds		$_____ -

(a)

Initial carrying value of bonds	$	-
Effective interest rate	X	0.04
Effective interest cost	$	-
Less cash paid (3% X $1,000,000)		-
Amortization for Jan. 1 to June 30, 20X5	$	-
Plus: Carrying value before periodic amortization		-
Revised carrying value as of June 30, 20X5	$	-
Effective interest rate	X	0.04
Effective interest cost	$	-
Less cash paid (3% X $1,000,000)		-
Amortization for July 1 to Dec. 31, 20X5	$	-
Plus: Carrying value before periodic amortization		-
Revised carrying value as of Dec. 31, 20X5	$	-
Effective interest rate	X	0.04
Effective interest cost	$	-
Less cash paid (3% X $1,000,000)		-
Amortization for Jan. 1 to June 30, 20X6	$	-
Plus: Carrying value before periodic amortization		-
Revised carrying value as of June 30, 20X6	$	-
Effective interest rate	X	0.04
Effective interest cost	$	-
Less cash paid (3% X $1,000,000)		-
Amortization for July 1 to Dec. 31, 20X6	$	-
Plus: Carrying value before periodic amortization		-
Revised carrying value as of Dec. 31, 20X6	$	-

(b)

GENERAL JOURNAL				
Date	Accounts		Debit	Credit
31-Dec				
31-Dec				

(c)

Periodic interest payments ($1,000,000 X 3%)	$ -	
Present value factor (16-period annuity, 2.5%)	X _____ -	$ -
Maturity value	$ 1,000,000	
Present value factor (16 periods, 2.5%)	X _____ -	$ -
Price of bond at 5%, 8 years to maturity		$ -

Basic Worksheets

	Term	Advantage/Disadvantage
The ability of a company to raise capital by issuing shares to the public	Publicly Traded	Advantage
The ability of an existing shareholder to sell shares without corporate approval		
The ability of the government to tax corporate earnings and dividends		
Periodic regulatory filings		
The ability of different individuals to pool resources		
The inability of creditors to pursue individual shareholders		
The life of the entity can exceed the life of the shareholders		

	Common	Preferred
The stock is described as 6%, cumulative		✓
The stock includes voting rights		
The stock is last in line in the event of liquidation		
The stock is convertible		
The stock ordinarily pays a fixed dividend		
The stock may be subject to significant appreciation		
The stock has a "call price"		
The stock has a mandatory redemption date		

GENERAL JOURNAL			
Date	Accounts	Debit	Credit
(a)			
	To record issue of 100,000 shares of $1 par value common stock at $30 per share		
(b)			
	To record issue of 50,000 shares of no par value common stock at $10 per share		
(c)			
	To record issue of 40,000 shares of $100 par value preferred stock at $102 per share		
(d)			
	To record issue of 5,000 shares of $5 par value common stock for land with a fair value of $75,000		

(a)

GENERAL JOURNAL				
Date	**Accounts**		**Debit**	**Credit**
Declare Date				
Record Date				
Pay Date				

(b)

(c)

(d)

(a)

(b)

(c)

(a)

(b), (c), (d)

GENERAL JOURNAL				
Date	**Accounts**		**Debit**	**Credit**
A				
	To record acquisition of 250,000 treasury shares at $10 per share			
B				
	To record reissue of 125,000 treasury shares at $17 per share			
C				
	To record reissue of 125,000 treasury shares at $6 per share			

(e)

(a)

Common stock,	$	-
Paid-in capital in excess of par		-
Retained earnings		-
Total stockholders' equity	$	-

(b)

Common stock,	$	-
Paid-in capital in excess of par		-
Retained earnings		-
Total stockholders' equity	$	-

(c)

Common stock,	$	-
Paid-in capital in excess of par		-
Retained earnings		-
Total stockholders' equity	$	-

(d)

GENERAL JOURNAL				
Date	Accounts		Debit	Credit
split				
small				
large				

The statement of stockholders' equity

	Common Stock, $1 Par	Paid-in Capital in Excess of Par	Retained Earnings	Treasury Stock	Total Stockholders' Equity
Balance on January 1	$ -	$ -	$ -	$ -	$ -
	-	-	-	-	-
	-	-	-	-	-
	-	-	-	-	-
				-	
	-	-	-	-	-
Balance on December 31	$ -	$ -	$ -	$ -	$ -

Involved Worksheets

(a)

DEBT OPTION:

BRANFORD CORPORATION Balance Sheet August 15, 20X4		
Assets		
Cash		$ -
Accounts receivable		250,000
Inventory		750,000
Property, plant, & equipment (net)		860,000
Total assets		$ -
Liabilities		
Accounts payable	$ 125,000	
Accrued liabilities	260,000	
Notes payable	-	
Total liabilities		$ -
Stockholders' equity		
Common stock, $5 par	$ -	
Paid-in capital in excess of par	-	
Retained earnings	310,000	
Total stockholders' equity		-
Total liabilities and equity		$ -

COMMON STOCK OPTION:

BRANFORD CORPORATION
Balance Sheet
August 15, 20X4

Assets

Cash		$ -
Accounts receivable		250,000
Inventory		750,000
Property, plant, & equipment (net)		860,000
Total assets		$ -

Liabilities

Accounts payable	$ 125,000	
Accrued liabilities	260,000	
Notes payable	-	
Total liabilities		$ -

Stockholders' equity

Common stock, $5 par	$ -	
Paid-in capital in excess of par	-	
Retained earnings	310,000	
Total stockholders' equity		-
Total liabilities and equity		$ -

NONCUMULATIVE PREFERRED STOCK OPTION:

BRANFORD CORPORATION
Balance Sheet
August 15, 20X4

Assets

Cash		$ -
Accounts receivable		250,000
Inventory		750,000
Property, plant, & equipment (net)		860,000
Total assets		$ -

Liabilities

Accounts payable	$ 125,000	
Accrued liabilities	260,000	
Notes payable	-	
Total liabilities		$ -

Stockholders' equity

Preferred stock, 8% noncumulative	$ -	
Common stock, $5 par	-	
Paid-in capital in excess of par	-	
Retained earnings	310,000	
Total stockholders' equity		-
Total liabilities and equity		$ -

CUMULATIVE PREFERRED STOCK OPTION:

BRANFORD CORPORATION **Balance Sheet** **August 15, 20X4**		
Assets		
Cash		$ -
Accounts receivable		250,000
Inventory		750,000
Property, plant, & equipment (net)		860,000
Total assets		$ -
Liabilities		
Accounts payable	$ 125,000	
Accrued liabilities	260,000	
Notes payable	-	
Total liabilities		$ -
Stockholders' equity		
Preferred stock, 6% cumulative	$ -	
Common stock, $5 par	-	
Paid-in capital in excess of par	-	
Retained earnings	310,000	
Total stockholders' equity		-
Total liabilities and equity		$ -

CONVERTIBLE PREFERRED STOCK OPTION:

BRANFORD CORPORATION **Balance Sheet** **August 15, 20X4**		
Assets		
Cash		$ -
Accounts receivable		250,000
Inventory		750,000
Property, plant, & equipment (net)		860,000
Total assets		$ -
Liabilities		
Accounts payable	$ 125,000	
Accrued liabilities	260,000	
Notes payable	-	
Total liabilities		$ -
Stockholders' equity		
Preferred stock, 4% convertible/cumulative	$ -	
Common stock, $5 par	-	
Paid-in capital in excess of par	-	
Retained earnings	310,000	
Total stockholders' equity		-
Total liabilities and equity		$ -

(b)

(c)

(d)

(e)

(f)

	20X1	20X2	20X3	20X4	Totals
Total Income/Dividends	$300,000	-0-	$900,000	$1,800,000	$3,000,000

If 3% Cumulative:

    Preferred dividends

    Common dividends

If 4% Noncumulative:

    Preferred dividends

    Common dividends

	Total Equity	Common Stock/ Preferred Stock	Additional Paid-in Capital	Treasury Stock	Retained Earnings
Issue common stock at par	▲	▲	N/C	N/C	N/C
Issue common stock at > par					
Issue preferred stock at par					
Issue preferred stock at > par					
Buy treasury stock (cost method)					
Resell treasury stock > cost (cost method)					
Resell treasury stock < cost (cost method)					
Declare cash dividend					
Pay previously declared cash dividend					
Declare and issue large stock dividend					
Declare and issue small stock dividend (fair value > par)					
Declare and issue stock split					

Journal entries and statement of stockholders' equity

(a)

GENERAL JOURNAL				
Date	**Accounts**		**Debit**	**Credit**
	Cash		2,000,000	
	Common Stock			600,000
	Pd-in Cap in Excess of Par - CS			1,400,000
	To record issuance of 200,000 shares of $3 par value common stock at $10 per share			
A				
B				
C				
D				

GENERAL JOURNAL

Date	Accounts		Debit	Credit
E				
F				
G				
H				

(b)

Dry Dock Container Corporation
Statement of Stockholders' Equity
For the Year Ending December 31, 20X5

	Preferred Stock, $100 Par	Common Stock, $3 Par	Paid-in Capital in Excess of Par - PS	Paid-in Capital in Excess of Par - CS	Retained Earnings	Treasury Stock	Total Stock-holders' Equity
Balance - January 1	$ -	$ -	$ -	$ -	$ -	$ -	$ -
Issue common shares	-	-	-	-	-	-	-
Issue preferred shares	-	-	-	-	-	-	-
Purchase treasury stock	-	-	-	-	-	-	-
Cash dividends	-	-	-	-	-	-	-
Reissue treasury stock	-	-	-	-	-	-	-
Net income	-	-	-	-	-	-	-
Stock dividend	-	-	-	-	-	-	-
Balance on December 31	$ -	$ -	$ -	$ -	$ -	$ -	$ -

(c)

Stockholders' Equity

Capital stock:

   Preferred stock, $ -

   Common stock,   - $ -

Additional paid-in capital: $ -

                                       -      -

   Total paid-in capital $ -

                                       $ -

Total stockholders' equity $ -

The legible statement of stockholders' equity follows:

	Preferred Stock, $50 Par	Common Stock, $2 Par	Capital in Excess of Par - PS	Paid-in Capital in Excess of Par - CS	Retained Earnings	Treasury Stock	Total Stock-holders' Equity
Paloma Corporation **Statement of Stockholders' Equity** **For the Year Ending December 31, 20X7**							
Balance on January 1	$ -	$ -	$ -	$ -	$ -	$ -	$ -
Issuance of common	-	-	-	-	-	-	-
Issuance of preferred	-	-	-	-	-	-	-
Purchase treasury stock	-	-	-	-	-	-	-
Net income	-	-	-	-	-	-	-
Preferred cash dividends	-	-	-	-	-	-	-
Common cash dividends	-	-	-	-	-	-	-
Stock dividend	-	-	-	-	-	-	-
Balance on December 31	$ -	$ -	$ -	$ -	$ -	$ -	$ -

Answers to the specific questions follow:

If 10,000 preferred shares were issued, what was the per share par value and issue price? Par value = ; Issue price =

Assuming the preferred dividend reflected a full-year amount at the normal yield, what is the percentage rate associated with preferred stock?

What price per share was received for the newly issued common shares?

How much was the aggregate price paid for the treasury stock purchase?

How many common shares were issued as of December 31?

What was the market price per share on the date of the stock dividend?

Name of business:

Product or service:

Operating history:

Type and features of security offered for sale:

Planned utilization of funds raised by security offering:

Basic Worksheets

Correction of an error - entry and reporting	B-15.01

(a)

GENERAL JOURNAL				
Date	**Accounts**		**Debit**	**Credit**
Mar. 20X4				

(b)

(c)

(a)

TRENCH COAT
Income Statement
For the Year Ending December 31, 20X8

(b)

TRENCH COAT
Income Statement
For the Year Ending December 31, 20X8

MELANIE MIELKE CONSTRUCTION COMPANY
Income Statement
For the Year Ending December 31, 20XX

Sales		$	-
Cost of goods sold			-
Gross profit		$	-
Operating expenses			
	$	-	
		-	
		-	-
Loss from continuing operations before tax benefit		$	-
Income tax benefit from operating loss			-
Net loss		$	-
Other comprehensive income			
	$	-	
		-	
			-
Comprehensive income		$	-

Three of the following statements are patently false. Find the three false statements. The other statements are true, and may include additional insights beyond those mentioned in the textbook.

"Earnings" is synonymous with "income from continuing operations plus or minus the effects of any discontinued operations."

Changes in accounting estimates must be reported by retrospective adjustment.

EBIT and EBITDA are accounting values that are required to be reported on the face of the income statement.

Other comprehensive income can be reported on the face of a statement of comprehensive income or in a separate reconciliation.

When there is reported change in value for available for sale securities, "comprehensive income" becomes synonymous with "net income."

Book value per share is an amount related to shares of common stock.

(a)

Time Interval	Portion of Year	Shares Outstanding During Time Interval	Calculations	Weighted-Average Impact
	12 months			0

(b)

(c)

(d)

	Earnings Per Share	Dividends Per Share	Market Price Per Share	Average Annual Increase in Earnings
Andrews Corporation	$2.50	$0.00	$25.00	5%
Borger Corporation	$1.00	$1.00	$18.00	10%
Calvert Corporation	$5.00	$2.50	$20.00	5%
Dorchester Corporation	$1.25	$0.00	$10.00	25%
Easton Corporation	$2.50	$0.75	$50.00	30%
Flores Corporation	$2.00	$0.10	$25.00	20%
Gerber Corporation	$0.10	$0.00	$ 5.00	10%
Houston Corporation	$0.50	$0.25	$20.00	3%

	P/E Ratio	PEG Ratio	Dividend Rate	Dividend Payout Ratio
Formula	Market price divided by EPS			
Andrews Corporation	10.00			
Borger Corporation				
Calvert Corporation				
Dorchester Corporation				
Easton Corporation				
Flores Corporation				
Gerber Corporation				
Houston Corporation				

Brazil Corporation:

Chile Corporation:

Return on assets and return on equity   B-15.09

	Net Income	Interest Expense*	Preferred Dividends	Average Assets	Average Equity
Alejando Corp.	$120,000	$10,000	$0	$1,100,000	$1,000,000
Ling Corp.	$100,000	$80,000	$20,000	$1,900,000	$1,100,000
Beaufort Corp.	$700,000	$200,000	$15,000	$4,000,000	$2,000,000
Robinson Corp.	$300,000	$200,000	$100,000	$6,000,000	$4,000,000

	Return on Assets	Return on Equity
Alejando Corp.		
Ling Corp.		
Beaufort Corp.		
Robinson Corp.		

Discussion:

(a) Deviations in measured outcomes from period to period should be the result of deviations in underlying performance (not accounting quirks).

(b) Clear and concise to those with reasonable business knowledge

(c) Available in sufficient time to be capable of influence.

(d) Even though different companies may use different accounting methods, there is still sufficient basis for valid comparison.

(e) Information must be truthful; complete, neutral, and free from error.

(f) Information should be timely and bear on the decision-making process by possessing predictive or confirmatory (feedback) value.

(g) Different knowledgeable and independent observers reach similar conclusions.

This organization is viewed as centric to the coordination of global harmonization of accounting standards.

This organization passed "Section 404" requiring public companies to implement a robust system of internal control.

This organization is the primary private-sector accounting rule-making body in the U.S.

This organization is no longer in existence, but once issued "opinions" on acceptable accounting practices.

This organization is a professional association of accountants who are seeking to advance the practice of accounting.

This organization was created many years ago, and it is charged with administration of laws that regulate the reporting practices of companies whose stock is publicly traded.

This organization is charged with overseeing the auditors of public companies.

(a)   Overcomes mixing alternative measurements into the financial statements.

(b)   A continuous business process can be segmented into discrete intervals.

(c)   Provides for an orderly allocation of costs and revenues over extended time periods.

(d)   Justification for consolidating the accounts of separate legal entities.

(e)   Because of this, changing currency values due to inflation effects are disregarded.

(a)   The currency of the country in which a subsidiary operates.

(b)   The anticipated direction of global GAAP development.

(c)   The world-wide equivalent of the FASB.

(d)   The currency of the country in which financial statements are prepared for owners.

(e)   Conversion process that uses a variety of exchange rates for assets.

(f)   The "plug" adjustment is an item of "other comprehensive income."

Foreign currency transactions - purchasing activity

GENERAL JOURNAL				Page	
Date	Accounts		Debit	Credit	
5-Dec					
11-Jan					

GENERAL JOURNAL				Page	
Date	Accounts		Debit	Credit	
5-Dec					
31-Dec					
11-Jan					

GENERAL JOURNAL				Page
Date	Accounts		Debit	Credit
5-Dec				
11-Jan				

GENERAL JOURNAL				Page
Date	Accounts		Debit	Credit
5-Dec				
31-Dec				
11-Jan				

Involved Worksheets

(a)

	$ -
	-
	$ -
	$ -
	-
	-
	$ -
	-
	$ -
	$ -
	-
	-
	$ -

(b)

(c)

(a)

Time Interval	Portion of Year	Shares Outstanding During Time Interval	Calculations	Weighted-Average Impact
Jan. 1 through June 30				
July 1 through Sept. 30				
Oct. 1 through Dec. 31				
	12 months			

(b)

Maximum price based on a P/E ratio of 15:

Maximum price based on a price to book value of 3:

Maximum price based on a minimum dividend yield of 3%:

A

GENERAL JOURNAL			Page	
Date	**Accounts**		**Debit ($)**	**Credit ($)**
1-Mar				
	Sold on account			
1-Apr				
	Collected account			
1-Apr				
	Sold on account			
1-May				
	Collected account			
1-May				
	Purchase on account			
1-Jun				
	Paid on account			
1-Jun				
	Purchase on account			
1-Jul				
	Paid on account			

B

| GENERAL JOURNAL | | | Page | |
Date	Accounts		Debit (£)	Credit (£)
1-Mar				
	Purchase on account			
1-Apr				
	Paid on account			
1-Apr				
	Purchase on account			
1-May				
	Paid on account			
1-May				
	Sold on account			
1-Jun				
	Collected account			
1-Jun				
	Sold on account			
1-Jul				
	Collected account			

Basic Worksheets

	Sub A	Sub B	Sub C
Cash	$ 1,000,000	$ 3,000,000	$ 5,000,000
Trading securities	3,000,000	2,000,000	1,000,000
Accounts receivable	6,000,000	5,000,000	14,000,000
Quick Assets	$ -	$ -	$ -
Inventory	4,000,000	8,000,000	7,000,000
Prepaid rent	2,000,000	2,000,000	3,000,000
Current Assets	$ -	$ -	$ -
Accounts payable	$ 5,000,000	$ 2,000,000	$ 8,000,000
Interest payable	1,000,000	1,000,000	6,000,000
Note payable (due in 6 months)	4,000,000	1,500,000	4,000,000
Unearned revenues	3,000,000	500,000	2,000,000
Current Liabilities	$ -	$ -	$ -

QUICK RATIO
(quick assets ÷ current liabilities)

CURRENT RATIO
(current assets ÷ current liabilities)

IMPORTED DATA:

Applicant	Total Liabilities	Paid-in Capital	Retained Earnings	Net Income for Past Year	Taxes for Past Year
Berkley	5,000,000	2,000,000	2,000,000	1,000,000	250,000
Costnor	2,500,000	1,000,000	500,000	400,000	100,000
Dalia	3,000,000	400,000	5,200,000	500,000	110,000
Fergusen	500,000	700,000	3,500,000	800,000	90,000
Hernandez	2,000,000	200,000	700,000	600,000	75,000
Indio	1,600,000	1,200,000	8,000,000	250,000	50,000
Jordanson	4,400,000	5,000,000	(400,000)	(60,000)	-
Kervin	3,000,000	1,500,000	1,800,000	10,000	1,000
Lensmire	600,000	500,000	500,000	250,000	60,000

CALCULATIONS:

	Debt to Total Assets	Debt to Equity	Times Interest Earned
Berkley			
Costnor			
Dalia			
Fergusen			
Hernandez			
Indio			
Jordanson			
Kervin			
Lensmire			

(a)

Accounts Receivable Turnover Ratio
=
Net Credit Sales/Average Net Accounts Receivable
=

(b)

Inventory Turnover Ratio
=
Cost of Goods Sold/Average Inventory
=

(c)

(a)

Sales	$	-
Cost of goods sold		-
Gross profit	$	-
Selling, general & administrative		-
Net income	$	-

(b)

Return on Assets Ratio

=

(Net Income + Interest Expense)

÷

Average Assets

=

Return on Equity Ratio

=

(Net Income - Preferred Dividends)

÷

Average Common Equity

=

Demonstrating understanding of P/E, book value, and yields   *B-16.05*

(a)

(b)

(a) Issue common stock for land   Non-cash investing/financing activity

(b) Issue common stock for cash

(c) Pay interest on loan

(d) Sell goods for cash

(e) Pay employee salaries

(f) Pay dividends to common shareholders

(g) Receive dividend on an investment

(h) Obtain proceeds of long-term loan

(i) Acquire treasury shares

(j) Purchase land for cash

(k) Buy inventory for resale

Cash flows from operating activities:

Cash received from customers $ -

Less cash paid for:

$ -

-

-

Net cash provided by operating activities $ -

Cash flows from operating activities:

Net income		$	-
Add (deduct) noncash effects on operating income			
	$	-	
		-	
		-	
		-	-
Net cash provided by operating activities		$	129,000

HERMAN CORPORATION
Statement of Cash Flows
For the year ending December 31, 20X2

Rearranging cash flows in good form - indirect approach

RIMMEREX CORPORATION
Statement of Cash Flows
For the year ending December 31, 20X5

Cash flows from operating activities:

Cash flows from investing activities:

Cash flows from financing activities:

Net increase in cash	$	-
Cash balance at January 1, 20X5		-
Cash balance at December 31, 20X5	$	-

Noncash investing/financing activities:

	$	-

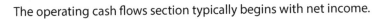

The operating cash flows section typically begins with net income.

Indirect

Separate disclosure is provided for noncash investing/financing activities.

Requires supplemental disclosure reconciling net income to operating cash flows.

Conceptually, the preferred approach.

Includes three separate sections - operating, investing, and financing.

Requires supplemental disclosure of cash paid for interest and cash paid for taxes.

A loss on the sale of a plant asset would be added back in operating cash flows.

OZARK CORPORATION
Statement of Cash Flows (Direct Approach)
For the year ending December 31, 20X5

Cash flows from operating activities:

Cash received from customers $ -

Less cash paid for:

   Merchandise inventory $ -

   Selling and administrative expenses   -

   Interest   -

   Income taxes   -   -

     Net cash provided by operating activities $ -

Cash flows from investing activities:

Purchase of equipment $ -

   Net cash used by investing activities   -

Cash flows from financing activities:

Proceeds from issuing stock $ -

Dividends on common   -

   Net cash provided by financing activities   -

Net decrease in cash $ -

Cash balance at January 1, 20X5   -

Cash balance at December 31, 20X5 $ -

Cash received from customers:

Cash paid for inventory:

Cash paid for selling and admin.:

Cash paid for interest:

Cash paid for income taxes:

OZARK CORPORATION
Statement of Cash Flows (Indirect Approach)
For the year ending December 31, 20X5

Cash flows from operating activities:

Net income		$ -
Add (deduct) noncash effects on operating income		
Depreciation expense	$ -	
Increase in accounts receivable	-	
Decrease in inventory	-	
Increase in prepaid insurance	-	
Decrease in accounts payable	-	
Decrease in interest payable	-	
Increase in income taxes payable	-	-
Net cash provided by operating activities		$ -

Cash flows from investing activities:

Purchase of equipment	$ -	
Net cash used by investing activities		-

Cash flows from financing activities:

Proceeds from issuing stock	$ -	
Dividends on common	-	
Net cash provided by financing activities		-
Net decrease in cash		$ -
Cash balance at January 1, 20X5		-
Cash balance at December 31, 20X5		$ -

Involved Worksheets

Ratios from comprehensive financial statements	*I-16.01*

Current Ratio | 4.70
| Current Assets ÷ Current Liabilities | $940,000 ÷ $200,000 |

Quick Ratio

Debt to Total Assets Ratio

Debt to Total Equity Ratio

Times Interest Earned Ratio

Accounts Receivable Turnover Ratio

Inventory Turnover Ratio

Net Profit on Sales

Gross Profit Margin

Return on Assets

Return on Equity

EPS

P/E

Dividend Rate/Yield

Dividend Payout Ratio

Book Value Per Share

TRAVIS ENGINEERING
Statement of Cash Flows
For the year ending December 31, 20X3

Cash flows from operating activities:

$ -

$ -

-

-

-

-                    -

$ -

Cash flows from investing activities:

$ -

-

-

Cash flows from financing activities:

$ -

-

-

Net increase in cash	$ -
Cash balance at January 1, 20X3	145,300
Cash balance at December 31, 20X3	$ -

Noncash investing/financing activities

$ -

Reconciliation of net income to cash flows from operating activities:

Net income $ 390,200

Add (deduct) noncash effects on operating income

	$	-
		-
		-
		-
		-
		-
	-	-
Net cash provided by operating activities	$	-

FRED SLEZAK CORPORATION
Statement of Cash Flows
For the year ending December 31, 20X5

Cash flows from operating activities:

$ -

$ -

-

-

-

-

-

-     -

$ -

Cash flows from investing activities:

$ -

-

Cash flows from financing activities:

$ -

-

-

Net increase in cash	$ -
Cash balance at January 1, 20X5	9,000
Cash balance at December 31, 20X5	$ -

Noncash investing/financing activities:

$ -

Supplemental information:

$ -

-

(a)

		LIVE OAK CORPORATION Cash Flow Statement Worksheet For the Year Ending December 31, 20X5		
	20X4	**Debit**	**Credit**	**20X5**
Debits				
Cash	$ 9,000			$ 664,000
Accounts receivable	345,000			375,000
Inventory	160,000			150,000
Prepaid expenses	25,000			35,000
Land	400,000			300,000
Building	700,000			700,000
Equipment	450,000			530,000
	$2,089,000			$2,754,000
Credits				
Accumulated depreciation	$ 270,000			$300,000
Accounts payable	119,000			112,000
Interest payable	-			2,000
Long-term note payable	-			80,000
Common stock ($1 par)	600,000			700,000
Paid-in capital in excess of par	400,000			800,000
Retained earnings	700,000			760,000
	$2,089,000			$2,754,000
Cash flows from operating activities:				
Cash flows from investing activities:				
Cash flows from financing activities:				
Noncash investing/financing activities:				

(b)

LIVE OAK CORPORATION				
Statement of Cash Flows				
For the year ending December 31, 20X5				

Cash flows from operating activities:

$ -

$ -

-

-

-

-

-

-

- -

Net cash provided by operating activities $ -

Cash flows from investing activities:

$ -

Net cash provided by investing activities -

Cash flows from financing activities:

$ -

-

Net cash provided by financing activities -

Net increase in cash $ -

Cash balance at January 1, 20X5 9,000

Cash balance at December 31, 20X5 $ -

Noncash investing/financing activities:

$ -

Supplemental information:

Company name:

Direct or indirect?

Positive or negative operating cash flow?

Financial services sector?

Photo Credits

Cover
Creative Travel Projects/Shutterstock.com

Made in the USA
Monee, IL
21 January 2021